MW00947307

One School's Journey

The Path to Authentic and Engaging Learning Using Projects

Written By
Eleanor K. Smith
and
Margaret Pastor

Copyright © 2018 Eleanor K. Smith and Margaret Pastor

All rights reserved

ISBN: 1-978-2773-7-7

ISBN 13:978-1-9782-7737-3

We dedicate this book to our grandchildren.

May your education be authentic and engaging.

This is not a book of lesson plans. Our bias is that for true authentic teaching you cannot follow someone else's lesson plans. Authentic projects come from the heart and are adapted to meet the needs and interests of your students.

This book tells the story of our journey, as a public elementary school staff, as we set down the path to discover how to engage our students. What did not surprise us is that when children are engaged, they learn. And authentic projects engage the learner. Our hope is that you will find inspiration from what we discovered along the way.

Table of Contents

Foreword viii

One The Martian Colony Project 1
Overview

Two Your Honor: A Car Lot, a Spa, and a Groundhog 6
Open-Ended Projects

Three From Play to Projects 13
Developing an Early Foundation

Four Autographs Will Be Available After the Show.....................18
Ownership by Students

Five The Time Machine...25
Context of the Authentic Experience

Six It's a Bird, It's a Plane, No It's Super Teaching...................31
Learning Should be Fun

Seven Failure Is Not an Option, But It Should Be.....................36
Learning from Failure

Eight Quiet, Please, The Show Is About to Begin 43
Managing Student Behavior

Nine Light My Fire 50
Excited About Teaching Again

Ten May We Present 55
Sharing Projects

Eleven The Proof Is in the Pudding 60
Student Growth

Twelve OneSchoolsJourney@gmail.com 64
Problems We Haven't Totally Solved...Yet

Thirteen The Journey Continues 70
Summary

Afterword 74

Projects 76
    List of Projects 78
    Ways to Present Projects 81
    Resources for Projects 83

Acknowledgements 118

Photo Credits 119

About the Authors 120

FOREWORD

Driving home after school one day I noticed that the van in front of me had a car seat with a Disney video playing on the overhead monitor in front of it. Part of me thought, how sad that a child had to be entertained while simply driving around town. What happened to conversation between the parent and child? What happened to a child being able to self-entertain for the duration of a car ride? The other part of me was jealous that we didn't have that technology when I had young children. How much easier would running errands, and long car trips, have been?

The teacher in me was struck, however, with what the current generation of children were entering school exposed to on a daily basis. We were teaching children that expected to be constantly entertained and engaged at all times. These kids were literally teething on their parents' cell phones and not only had a comfort level, but an expectation of constant access to technology that held their interest. How could we as teachers compete?

Should we compete?

Or should we be embracing our students' abilities and expectations to be constantly engaged on a personal level? Isn't that what good teaching should be about?

The use of authentic projects to teach is not a new concept. If we look back at apprenticeships of centuries past, students were taught a real and useful trade by working in that trade. They didn't read books about it, they didn't study Cliffs Notes and take a written exam. They worked in the trade until they were deemed ready to go out and practice the trade. Skills were not taught in isolation. There was no wondering why something was being taught. It was meaningful and it was real.

This book will hopefully be a meaningful and real tool for your use as a classroom teacher, specialist, or administrator with a goal to engage your students and increase their academic achievement. And hopefully it will increase their quest for knowledge and love of learning as well.

We have had tremendous success with using authentic projects to teach in our elementary school, which is a very diverse school with high percentages of low income, English learner, and mobile students. Our school is in Maryland, in a suburb community of Washington, DC. Basically, we have a building full of students with diverse backgrounds and many different needs.

As the authors of this book, we bring two very different perspectives on what is, and what should be, going on in a classroom. I very recently retired from the school this book is based on. (Only a retired teacher would actually have time to write a book.) I was the special education resource teacher. I co-taught in the classrooms and helped create several authentic projects, with several different classroom teachers, that were hugely successful. The other author of this book is the school's principal. (I have no idea how she had time to write a book.) It was her idea to bring authentic projects into the school.

Unless otherwise annotated, the rest of this book has been written by both of us. Our goal is not to give you lesson plans that you can use in the classroom as, honestly, that is not true authentic teaching. True authentic teaching needs to involve a project that is exciting to both the teacher and the students, be an open-ended idea that motivates the teacher and students to explore and grow as learners, has real world applications, and be something that grabs everyone's attention and doesn't let go. Our hope is to give you some "food for thought." We will share stories about what worked for us and hope that you will have that "epiphany" of what might work for you.

Chapter One

The Martian Colony Project

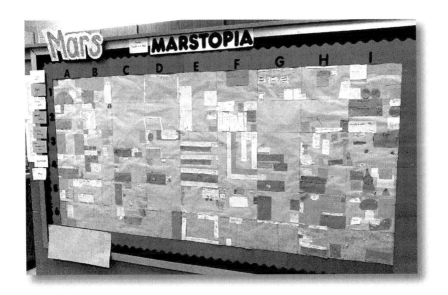

The Martian Colony Project started by accident. And it accidentally solved many of the problems that our teachers were facing in fifth grade. It started the year that our school was beginning to explore the use of teaching using authentic projects.

On a hot Friday afternoon in September, the teachers were faced with a classroom full of overheated fifth-graders who had just returned from recess, and who were not the least bit interested in the math lesson that was planned. This classroom had not only learners significantly above grade level, but also English language (ESOL) learners and special education students.

Engaging fifth-graders is always difficult. Meeting all of their diverse needs is almost impossible. Add to the mix the heat and the end of the school week and it became obvious that the planned math lesson was not going to happen.

The National Aeronautics and Space Administration (NASA) had just posted some new videos online about their latest Martian rovers. The teachers decided to show these videos to the students instead of the planned math lesson. The students were totally hooked and the class spent the rest of the afternoon talking about what was going on with the exploration of Mars.

The following Monday afternoon, the staff meeting was a discussion of beginning authentic projects and how a hook was needed to engage the students. The fifth-grade teachers realized that they had found that hook with the NASA videos. What they did not know was what to do with this. At this point they decided to go with "Martian Friday" where they would spend Friday afternoons learning about Mars and space exploration.

Realizing that they needed to use those precious class hours to continue with fifth-grade curriculum, the teachers began to plan how to incorporate math and science goals into "Martian Friday." They quickly discovered that many curriculum goals could be easily adapted. The study of the Solar System, matter, motion, energy, and more, easily jumped right into the project. Math goals such as computation, area, and time were also easily incorporated. Reading and writing naturally worked into the project. (There were problems with the order in which the teachers wanted to work on goals not necessarily matching up with the order of the fifth-grade curriculum - more on that later.)

This went on for several weeks and the students continued to be very excited about Mars. The teachers then came up with the idea of having the class design a Martian colony. They divided a bulletin board into six-inch by nine-inch "pods" using a scale of one-inch to one-foot. Students taped a six-foot by nine-foot area on the classroom floor to demonstrate the limited space in each pod. Each student and both teachers were assigned their own pod. The remaining pods were designated for the technology needed to support life in the colony. The class developed a key using colored index cards and students "furnished" their pods.

The colony quickly became "real" to students as they researched and designed their own Martian colony. Students gravitated to the colony bulletin board throughout the school day.

Much of the teaching was now guided by "casual" student discourse while they worked on the pods. Questions and dialogue flowed, and the teachers incorporated academic content into these student-led and student-owned conversations.

As the class moved into what would be needed to survive on Mars, the science lessons multiplied exponentially. Students posted their ideas on an "Idea Board," which was modeled after a picture of a whiteboard the class had seen in the background of a photo from the Mars Science Laboratory at NASA's Jet Propulsion Laboratory. Students also began incorporating personal interests into the colony. Surveys, supply lists, expense forms, and descriptive proposals filled the "Idea Board." Without planning this, "Martian Friday" had slowly expanded to include the rest of the week.

The year ended with the formation of a student-created Martian colony government. The students held elections and then drafted a constitution for their colony. The teachers were now able to incorporate many curriculum goals from the formation of the United States government into the formation of the Martian Colony government. Even the concept of "colony" was readily and heavily reinforced by the planned colonization of Mars.

Armed with what they had learned, the teachers decided to expand the project the following year. The beginning of the year was spent front-loading the students with knowledge about Earth, Mars, the solar system, and space exploration. Throughout the year, the students continued to read about Earth, Mars, and space in reading groups. They teleconferenced with space scientists and had guest speakers with expertise in geography and space exploration. They watched videos about Earth, Mars, and space. They took field trips, including a trip to the Smithsonian Air and Space Museum.

The students built a life-size model of one of the living pods. They collected boxes and used many of the fifth-grade math goals to construct a prototype pod. Students simultaneously created and displayed science experiments developed for the International Space Station and Mars in a Virtual Science Fair. The entire student body, parents, and many community members were invited to view the projects at an end-of-year event.

Every year the Martian Colony Project grew and became more comprehensive. Each year the teachers recognized more ways to incorporate academic curriculum into the project. The fifth-grade poetry unit became a vehicle for the creation of poetry about Mars and space, which was displayed in the prototype Martian colony classroom. Area and perimeter were taught while laying out the floor plan for the prototype pod. United States and world history were tied into the creation of the new Martian government. The curriculum tie-ins became fluid and endless.

Student achievement also rose each year. Students were able to work at their own academic level. ESOL students had a real context to expand their mastery of the English language, and since they were actively working with peers, there was far more real dialogue. The special education students were able to experience achievement and success exploring advanced concepts on their academic level.

One young man, both an ESOL and special education student, came to our school in fourth grade as a non-reader with a history of behavior problems. He initially participated minimally in class. This began to change with his exposure to a geography project in fourth grade. He left at the end of fifth grade reading at a second-grade level. While still significantly below grade level, he was experiencing academic growth and success for the first time.

After a class discussion about the difficulty of returning to Earth from Mars due to the need for fuel to be available on Mars for the return trip, this young man proposed a possible solution. The formerly sullen, non-engaged student proposed that the class build and launch the pods from the moon since the lower gravity of the moon would mean rockets would use less fuel to launch and have more left for a possible return trip to Earth. He was delighted when shown current articles from NASA where aerospace engineers were considering just such a proposal. This from a child who teachers thought might need a more supportive special education placement when he arrived in fourth grade.

High achievers were also forced to leave their comfort zones of being able to fill out a worksheet or pass a test with correct answers, since much of what they were exploring did not have one correct answer.

During the fall design phase of the Martian colony living pods, one high achiever sought the co-teacher out to complain that her perfectly measured and scaled furnishings did not fit in her pod. Upon investigation, she realized her pod was one half-inch short. (She actually tracked the co-teacher down in another classroom, politely interrupted what the teacher was doing, and gave her quite the lecture!) She continued to explain that this half-inch represented six inches in actual scale and that this was "a lot of space to lose." The co-teacher apologized but explained that this can happen in construction and that she would either have to work in the smaller space or change pods.

After several days of collaboration with other students, the student decided to keep her assigned pod but negotiated sharing part of her neighbor's pod. The math, science, and social language the students used in completing their work on the colony bulletin board, and in discussing their pods, exceeded what teachers had seen in previous fifth-grade classes.

The Martian Colony Project received several recognitions from NASA, including a spot on the NASA Explorer Schools Merit list. The students were thrilled, as this verified that they were working on projects that NASA recognized as real science. This was, of course, something that the formerly sullen, non-engaged, ESOL/ Special Education student - now class leader - already knew.

Chapter Two

Your Honor: A Car Lot, a Spa, and a Groundhog

Interviews for the position of general manager for the third-grade car lot took place several weeks into the Car Lot Project. This project started as a vehicle (pun intended) for the third-graders to learn about motion, friction, and speed by designing their own cars. Initially the teachers had hoped to cover several third-grade objectives in math and science.

It soon evolved into a full-fledged classroom-sized car lot, covering a multitude of third-grade curriculum goals, complete with model cars, detailed written Power Point presentations for each car, a sales office, and an employee break room.

The teachers listened to what the students were interested in and incorporated this into the project as it evolved. When it was brought up that the car lot needed a general manager, several students volunteered. It was decided that the students would interview for the position with the classroom teacher and co-teacher in front of the rest of the class. (This was a great way to pick up some speaking grades for the current report card, and the ESOL teacher also listened in to get some progress notes as well.) What a wonderful surprise when the two best interviews were given by two struggling students who had rarely had a chance to shine before. The class voted to have them co-manage the car lot.

During the design phase of the cars, the children were able to bring their own passions into the designs and construction of their cars. Cars featured refrigerators for food, microwaves, hot tubs, and even a mini batting cage. The sky was literally the limit, as several of the cars were designed to have the ability to fly.

Before the grand opening of the car lot, the students decided to film commercials about their cars. These commercials were written, produced, and performed by the students, filmed on the teacher's cell phone, and then shared with other classrooms before they visited the car lot. (This was another great way to pick up more speaking and writing grades. The special educator and speech pathologist were able to remediate and mark progress on several student objectives from these commercials as well.)

After the cars were presented to the school, parents, and community, they were raced against each other. This sequence of events was discussed, and it was decided that it was better to share the cars before they were raced, in case damage occurred during the race. (Smart decision - not all the cars survived this event.) Additional academic and curriculum goals were covered during this race portion including the measurement of length and time.

The success of the Car Lot, Martian Colony, and several other projects in our building, had us look at what made these projects work. What did these projects have in common that made them reach and engage our students?

One of the major elements we identified was that the most effective and engaging projects were open-ended. While the teachers had a starting point and goals that they wanted to achieve along the way, the projects were structured to allow students to engage in and explore what interested them. This was accomplished by the teachers listening, truly listening, to student discourse during work on the projects.

During the first year of the Martian Colony Project, a group of fifth-grade girls initially engaged with only minimal effort. (If you have spent any time with preteens, you know what minimal effort can look like, and it is not pretty!)

In a conversation with one of the teachers, the girls started asking about the availability of makeup and hair styling supplies on Mars. The initial topic was most likely brought up to get a reaction out of the teacher, and it did. It was decided that the girls would design a spa for the colony. This led to six months of extensive research and investigation into what would be needed to supply a spa on Mars.

At one point the girls proudly presented their supply requisition only to realize that they had two problems. They had only requisitioned one color of nail polish, and as it took nine months to get supplies from Earth, they did not have enough supplies to last until the next shipment arrived.

This led to the development of nail polish color preference surveys and the requisition of additional supplies. Then the problem of lack of storage space came up. The girls would solve one problem to encounter another. All problems required reading, writing, math, and social negotiations. The girls started staying in for recess to try to get a handle on problems with the spa. By the end of the year, the least engaged members of the class were the most engaged.

There was no way the teachers involved in the Martian Colony Project could have planned for the spa back in September. For the colonies that were completed in the following years, only one contained a spa. Subsequent colonies included a farm (more on that later), a soccer stadium, security sales office, and a government meeting room. None of these were planned in September. All came about from student interest.

Listening to what students are saying is critical to the implementation and success of projects when using authentic learning and teaching. Both the Car Lot and the Martian Colony would have been themed activities that achieved typical student engagement and growth without this component. Students, like teachers, bring varied interests, experiences, background knowledge, and academic levels into their learning. When authentic projects are open-ended, students are able to engage in a way that is meaningful to them.

This does not mean that the classroom teacher enters into the project with a vague idea of what needs to be accomplished. In actuality, the more specific the teacher is with academic goals and objectives, the easier it is to incorporate student ideas and interests.

In the fifth-grade classroom working on the Martian Colony Project, when it became apparent that the girls were very engaged when discussing the Martian spa, the teacher was able to refer to lesson plans for current academic goals and tie them into what the girls were discussing. For example, at the time the girls were deciding on nail polish color, a current fifth-grade objective involved fractions. During the girls' discussion on needed nail polish colors, fractions were inserted into the discourse by the classroom teacher.

The teacher was able to guide the girls into this math concept while listening to their discussions about the spa and use fractions as a tool to look at the needs of the spa. At the same time, another group was looking at creating a Martian football league. Again, fractions were used when discussing how to divide up the league.

This was not a hit or miss activity to incorporate curriculum into the open-ended projects. It required constant surveying of student interest by listening to what they were discussing, and then finding the way to best incorporate academic objectives into this discussion. While it may sound like more work for the classroom teacher, as the students were providing the framework and engagement for the lessons, it was easier for the teachers to instruct this way.

Another interesting example of the impact of being open to the voice of the students came from a fourth-grade classroom that was busy reading two different stories, both with a central theme of judging others unfairly. It began with the standard literacy objective of comparing and contrasting two works of literature. While discussing the reading, student questions and debate turned to how and where judgment happens, who has the right to judge, and why we judge. The next turn in the conversation led to courts of law and how they operate. The teacher, listening to this with care, proposed the idea of writing a case of their own as a class, using characters and situations from the readings, and then trying the case in their own mock court of law.

The class exploded with enthusiasm, and they were off on an authentic project where they wrote and researched at length. This culminated in the staging of a trial where each class member chose and prepared for a specific role in the case. Visitors were invited to sit in the courtroom gallery as audience members during the trial, and at the end the students responded to questions from the audience and solicited feedback.

As with the Car Lot Project and the Martian Colony Project, the Court Project, while curriculum driven, was also open-ended. This allowed the teacher to listen to what the students were interested in, concerned about, and motivated by, and move the project along accordingly.

One day in a kindergarten classroom, the students noticed the groundhogs at play outside the classroom window. Noting the students' fascination with the animals, the teacher set up an observation post with binoculars and over time the Groundhog Project was launched. This included a study of the seasons, habitats, life cycle, the math of population increase, and much more relating to groundhogs. Once again, student discourse moved the open-ended project along.

The following year the teacher was prepared to introduce the Groundhog Project in the beginning of the school year. But the children in this class never engaged like the children had the previous year. Even being better prepared and more engaged herself, the teacher did not see that "spark" of engagement from her students. In the four years that followed, the project was never pursued again, because the students did not demonstrate the curiosity to go forward.

The kindergarten teacher was so open to following student response that she was available to change direction to insure engagement. It should be noted that the teacher developed an entirely different project when she found that the students, while not interested in groundhogs, were very interested in a wide variety of other animals that worked well in authentic learning.

The classroom teacher and co-teacher involved in the Car Lot Project knew that they had several struggling students in this class. This was certainly incorporated into their discussions for meeting student academic needs, back-mapping, and scaffolding. What neither of them could have anticipated was the interest of two of these students in becoming the car lot manager and how much growth would take place during this part of the project.

This amazing transformation would not have happened without an open-ended project and a classroom teacher who listened and allowed these students to flourish by following their own interests. This also would not have happened if all of the adults in the room were not willing to listen and learn from each other, willing to support each other in the professional goals they needed to accomplish in their respective professional positions, and willing to leave their egos at the door.

The incredible thing is that when you do this, not only do the students flourish, but the classroom becomes a fun place to work.

Using co-teachers in the classroom is an integral part of how we have taught in our school. This has huge benefits, but also presents problems, especially for the co-teacher who has objectives that need to be met with caseload students. A nice benefit of teaching with open-ended projects was the ease with which I was able to meet special education goals in the classroom. Projects are geared to "make it real" and "make it count." Good special education goals have always been written this way. I found the transition to teaching using projects to be easy, exciting, and much better for my students. The benefits of having students receive additional services within the classroom, rather than pulling them out and disrupting their day, was another huge benefit, and probably another book!

-Ellie (Special Education Resource Teacher/Classroom Co-Teacher)

Chapter Three

From Play to Projects

A few years ago, at the end of the school year, the first grand opening and guided tour of an art gallery was held featuring some very special presenters. These students shared not only information about the featured artists, but also showcased their own work done in the style of each artist. The student artists/docents were enthusiastic and totally engaged in the presentation of their work.

The students and adults visiting the gallery learned about artistic styles including impressionism, cubism and modernism through the works of artists such as Monet, Van Gogh, Seurat, Picasso, and O'Keeffe.

Visitors left with a solid appreciation for different artists and their genres. The narrative shared by the docents was informative, complete, and not memorized but recited from their own personal accomplishment and experience with each artist. This extraordinary art gallery was created by, and the tours were given by, five-year-olds.

The kindergarten teacher who developed this project first began to explore the idea after visiting the Phillips Collection in Washington, DC. Shortly afterward she happened across a video in which teachers were discussing the power of words and pictures. This spurred her thinking about the place of art in learning and thus began the Art Gallery Project.

In the kindergarten art gallery class, the teacher began the year by exposing her students to one artist. The natural curiosity of these five-year-olds went in many directions. Color, form, and style were everywhere in their discussions. The students participated in group readings and writings about this artist. They explored the landscapes and physical themes of the art, and they used timelines to place the artist in history. They used math to explore the artist's age, number of works, and compared and contrasted this to other artists as the year progressed. This included using the mathematics of art to create space and perspective in everything from the linear measure of a picture frame to the pixel points within a space. The children also created art in the style of each artist.

As the gallery grew and changed over several years, the classroom teacher was able to incorporate more district curriculum into her gallery. She was also able to include more artists, exposing the children to increased diversity. After completing a project using recycled materials in the style of Nnenna Okore, the classroom teacher photographed the students' artistic interpretation and sent a copy to Ms. Okore. She responded that she was so impressed that she turned the photograph into a poster for her office.

In another kindergarten classroom, the teacher saw opportunity in the approach of fall and the chance to pick pumpkins at a nearby pumpkin patch. The children were so excited about the pumpkins that she began to explore with them what would happen when they cut the pumpkins open. The more the class worked on the pumpkins, the more questions they posed. Why did some pumpkins grow larger than others? Why were the colors different? Why were the shapes different? Did they all have the same number of seeds inside?

Finding these answers gave rise to wonderful reading, writing, math, and science opportunities. The more questions the children asked, the easier it became for the teacher to incorporate district curriculum into the search for answers in a meaningful, authentic way.

In a parent-included event, additional pumpkins were cut open, seeds counted and grouped, and circumference was measured with yarn. Results were charted and compared, and notes were made about their discoveries. Parents began to mention ways that they could follow up on this activity at home.

The earlier you start educating children this way, the more they will get out of the experience later. Students involved with authentic projects early in their education come to expect that there is more than one way to solve a problem, that collaborating with others is the best approach, and that persistence pays off. This is why we feel it is so important to start with authentic teaching the minute students enter school. It also sets the stage for seeing the learning experience as one of rich engagement and even joy, which is a necessary prerequisite for becoming a life-long learner.

As students become comfortable with learning this way, the classroom teacher will be able to delve ever deeper into the authentic learning world. The familiarity of the student with how it works allows the teacher to quickly move from a teacher-centered day to a student-centered day. While it is frequently pointed out that the preparation and front loading prior to the beginning of a project pays off in how it frees the teacher to respond to the students in the learning moment, those students who have been taught this way before can better add to the process as well.

Those students who are working with authentic projects for the first time after some years in school have to re-learn how to approach learning itself, and the older they are the more difficult this is. By the time children reach middle school, they have formed an idea of what schooling is that does not include exploration or personalization. At this point their expectation will be that learning is a means to a grade, seldom interesting, and rarely engaging or exciting. On the other hand, our youngest learners are predisposed to authentic learning as an adventure that feeds their natural curiosity.

Kindergarteners historically entered school needing to learn the building blocks of reading, writing, math, and social skills. While this is still true, we are dealing with a generation that is literally teething on technology. Babies in strollers are handed cell phones to entertain themselves as babies in the past were handed a pacifier. The entering kindergarteners are very comfortable with today's technology. We need to take this ability and thirst for information and expand it. These five-year-olds are prime candidates for authentic learning.

Along with the introduction of teaching using authentic projects, our school decided to hold student-led parent conferences in order to honor our mission of keeping the role of the student central in his or her learning. Kindergarten was the one grade where the teachers did not feel comfortable holding conferences in this form. They felt that the children were too young to productively explain their learning, especially in the first half of the school year. However, the projects usually culminated in an exhibition of the work to which the parents and other community members were invited.

Once the teachers became comfortable with project presentations, they found that even our youngest learners could capably speak of their own learning. These young students were more than able to hold student-led conferences with their parents.

The grandmother of one of the children who participated in the Art Gallery Project wrote a note to the teacher to tell her that she had learned about the project when her grandson, while thumbing through a coffee table book of artists at her home, began to tell her about the artists and how they created their art. He was so excited, and she was so surprised, that she made it a point to visit the classroom gallery herself.

In addition to having all staff, such as special education teachers, ESOL teachers, speech teachers and classroom assistants, work within the classroom rather than pulling children from the classroom, we had already established some other practices that eased the way to authentic projects. We used small group instruction, as opposed to whole group instruction, as the dominant way to teach everything. We addressed behavior problems as a one-on-one opportunity to reteach how and why we make choices. And as mentioned, we held student-led conferences with parents in which the students shared a portfolio of their work with their own parents, preparing ahead of time to talk about their successes and challenges. -Peggy (Principal)

Chapter Four

Autographs Will Be Available After the Show

I first heard about the Opera Project when I learned about a third-grade teacher transferring to our school. She was bringing the Opera Project with her. In all honesty, I thought it would be a huge failure. I could not exactly see our third-graders being the least bit interested or engaged in opera. I could not see myself being the least bit interested or engaged in opera. I was one-hundred percent wrong! -Ellie

The Opera Project was a year-long authentic learning experience developed to incorporate district curriculum with a student developed, written, produced, and directed production. The teacher was first inspired by an opera production she saw at another elementary school many years prior to coming to our school. While the opera she saw was an arts project, she envisioned using the opera as a vehicle for teaching an entire grade level curriculum.

With this idea in mind, she attended a teacher training program on opera that was being offered by the Metropolitan Opera Guild in New York City. The major purpose of this program was to expose school staff to opera. The hoped-for outcome was an increase in student experience with opera.

The teacher combined this idea with her previous experience with student written and produced plays to create her first opera with other staff in her school. She was then invited to share how she used opera to teach curriculum content by the Opera Guild at their summer program, and this in turn led to an invitation to do the same in Spain. During a sabbatical year in Spain, additional teacher training was developed and the program grew.

This was a huge journey, both intellectually and professionally, for this teacher. By the time she arrived at our school, she had many operas under her belt, and with the help and support of peers, had developed a truly authentic learning experience for her students.

When we realized how engaged the students were in the opera, we took a step back to figure out why. What was pulling these kids in? Why were they literally strutting around the building with their chests puffed out and their chins held high when they talked about what was going on in this classroom? Why in the world were our football fanatic, wrestling mania, video game loving students buying into opera, of all things?

We felt that one of the answers to all of these questions was ownership. The students owned the opera. They had written it, cast it, staged it, produced it, advertised it, and owned it. The decisions being made were theirs. Their interests, concerns, and dreams were being incorporated into their work. While we have yet to see a football themed opera, we have seen one set in an amusement park, a bowling alley, and our nearby nation's capital.

Watching this class in action made us realize another reason that authentic projects were being so successful in our building. When a child completes a reading assignment or a worksheet, the activity is owned by the teacher. In a sense, the learning belongs to that teacher.

At a previous school, I worked really hard getting ready for my annual observation. After the lesson, which went flawlessly, the principal made the following comment. "That was a great lesson. I can tell you put a lot of time into preparing for that. You learned a lot. I'm not so sure the kids got anything out of it, though." I was mad at him for a week. After I cooled off, I realized he was correct, but I wasn't sure how to fix this. Looking back, I realized I owned that lesson, but the kids didn't. -Ellie

Giving students - children - ownership can be difficult. With student ownership comes a new problem for the classroom teacher. That is the problem of letting go of control. That doesn't mean letting the students run wild with the project. It means letting them guide the teacher through the process through their interests, while the teacher still remains in control of the structures and the curriculum goals that need to be covered.

We've all seen the gorgeous bulletin boards up in a school hall. All the papers are perfect, they are all hanging in the same direction, spaced equally apart, with a beautiful caption on the top (using those lovely letters bought at the teacher supply store). Now imagine a bulletin board made and put up by children with what is important to them. The work is not perfect (more on that later), the papers are hanging in all different directions, the caption is written by a student and contains a spelling mistake. And the kids own this. It is theirs. They are proud of their work. They have internalized their work. They are learning.

And yes, it is extremely difficult not to cringe when other adults look at the bulletin board. You want to blurt out, "Hey, the kids did this. I know it's not perfect, and I know how to spell that misspelled word."

This, by the way, does not mean that we do not work on spelling words correctly. It means that spelling is incorporated into a learning context in which the student work is continually in process.

With ownership also comes the need to continue your work. We saw this phenomenon again and again. Children would come in on Monday morning very excited about something they had researched, read about, heard about, or created, that had to do with their project. As the students owned the project, and it was open-ended, they made connections to other things going on in their lives. Instead of being passive observers, they became active participants. The third-grade Opera Project certainly epitomized this concept. These students owned every aspect of the opera.

In a fourth-grade class that began with a nutrition focus, the students themselves questioned home-made versus factory-produced food. They decided to do a comparison and the Bake-Off Project began. The teacher and the counselor (the originator of a Gardening Project which emphasized fresh food and nutrition) worked together to help guide the experience by infusing research, writing, history and math into the project. The finale was the day that the children actually baked a cake that they made from scratch and another from a box mix. They had compared the two in terms of ingredients, nutrition, servings, and, finally, taste. Every child in the room felt the importance of what they did.

Another good example was the fifth-grade project titled "Hope and Fear." The teacher started the journey by sharing the art of Jacob Lawrence from his series "The Great Migration." It turned out to have special relevance to our students, many of whom had immigrated to this country and who saw themselves in the stories of migration.

When students can identify in some way with the project, ownership increases. The children gravitated to the music, poetry and art of the period and gave voice to their own migration stories through their writing, poetry and art. Whether students had stories of moving down the street, moving through a significant life event, or from one country to another, the ownership of the story was a driving force.

Relinquishing control to allow for student ownership is the truly scary part for the classroom teacher. Giving control of a script for a production that may be seen by an entire school is not an easy thing to do. However, by retaining total control, the teacher risks being the only person to truly learn and grow from the process. This is certainly not what our goal as educators should be.

Part of this problem is solved by starting small and taking baby steps. The teacher involved with the Opera Project did not present her first opera on a world class stage, she had initially written a class play that her students performed.

Putting on a student written, directed, and produced production is a brave thing for an educator to do. It is very difficult to not put your best foot forward at all times. Deep inside, we all want to present the quintessential perfect bulletin board, with all perfect papers, perfectly displayed in the perfect school hallway (if there is such a thing).

This ownership factor can also be seen when teachers correct papers and hand them back to students. Most students simply look at the grade. They have no ownership over the corrections on the paper. And then students are asked to copy the paper over or retype the paper, a laborious process for even the best keyboarder. If you go back and ask the students about the corrections they made, few if any can name the corrections. They rewrote it and got the teacher off their back. Check that box. No ownership of the final product. No learning.

So instead of an imperfect bulletin board full of real student work (not re-copied from teacher corrections), at all different levels of skill and achievement; imagine an imperfect opera, displayed in front of a school and community. Even performed on stage at the Kennedy Center in Washington, DC. Brave teacher!

When the opera was presented at the end of the school year, the teacher, other staff, and parents who had worked with the class, sat at the back of the room during the performances. One of the goals for the students was that if something went wrong during a performance, they could and would deal with the problem themselves. If a prop fell over or a cue was missed, adults did not rush in to fix it. The students took care of it. Imagine how hard it was for those adults to stay in the back of the room, waiting for a student fix to occur.

But the journey spoke for itself, in the previously mentioned pride of the students in their production. And the student growth and achievement spoke for itself with what these students accomplished over the year.

Adults who came to see the opera performed at the end of the school year frequently commented on how amazed they were that third-graders could create something that good. The truth is that the opera was not the best opera anyone had ever seen. The dialogue, music, and set were not "Madame Butterfly." The beauty lay in the fact that it was beyond what one would think that an eight-year-old was capable of producing, while at the same time the embedded learning was the kind that we think can only happen in a class of very gifted students.

The Opera and "Hope and Fear" were owned by the students. The products were theirs. The learning was theirs. And we are fairly confident that if we were to run into some of these students in thirty years, their memories about elementary school would not be about teacher owned lessons and worksheets, but about the student owned opera, migration, and other authentic projects. And the learning and confidence gained from these experiences would still be with them.

When I first tried to introduce authentic teaching and learning through projects at our school, we began the conversation at faculty meetings by talking about engaging the student as a focus of instruction. But it never seemed to have much real impact on what happened in the classroom. We were still being driven by, and focused on, covering a curriculum fast enough to (we thought) give our students the best chance to do well on the state tests.

It took awhile for teachers to engage in authentic teaching. But once staff saw the success of these projects, and the ownership of the projects by both staff and students, they began to truly engage in the process. -Peggy

Chapter Five

The Time Machine

I was working in one fifth-grade classroom when several students from another fifth-grade class rushed in. Their class was in the middle of a literature study of several authors, including Chris Van Allsburg. The cover of Van Allsburg's book, The Mysteries of Harris Burdick, showed four characters, all seated on a sail propelled rail car. The woman in the picture, seen from behind, looked exactly like, well, me! Slightly rounded (sadly true), middle-aged (yep), medium brown hair, wearing a dress (my usual attire), there I sat. The students then eagerly pointed out that the book was copyrighted in 1984. They knew my age and had figured out I was in my early twenties when I somehow ended up on the cover of this book as a middle-aged woman. They had also seen pictures of me figure skating in my twenties in the 1980's and knew that in 1984 I wasn't as rounded as I appeared now. Only one explanation: I had time traveled back to appear on the cover of this book. -Ellie

In *Back to the Future II*, Marty McFly returns to his present, from the past, and then goes on to the year 2015. If you followed that, then you would love to have been in the fifth-grade class doing the Time Machine Project. The fifth-grade teacher who created this engaging project came up with the idea in 2015 when the movie industry, and the fifth-grade teacher, were celebrating the arrival of the year portrayed in the movie in 1989. (Are you still following this?) This event, combined with the teacher's passion for the Revolutionary War Period, was the beginning of the Time Machine Project.

In a classroom where both teacher and students had become enthralled with the idea of what it would mean to travel through time, there was no end to the ways that learning could be incorporated (apparently, even including a literature study of Chris Van Allsburg). Of course, history could be incorporated into this project, but you needed math to end up in the right place in time, and science to know what could be used as fuel for a return to the present. To decide where you would go with your one chance to travel, well, you needed to research and study your options carefully.

Technology meant final student presentations included not only written journal entries about their trips into the past, but also pictures where the students could insert their own photos into historical photos or paintings. This helped to bring the student time travel trips to life when shared with others.

Once the students satisfied the initial requirement of learning about the Revolutionary War, they were then able to continue to study topics of choice. The students were able to explore just about any and all interests while meeting goals that the teacher had. You could become Dan Marino starting in his college years and ending with his chase of the elusive Super Bowl win with the Miami Dolphins. Figure skating? How about becoming Dorothy Hamill. Rocket Science? Maybe one of the women documented in *Hidden Figures*.

You could feel how personal the Time Machine Project was to the students by how excited they became working on this. They themselves recognized how much the engagement increases when the context of the learning is personal when they decided that one of the teachers had obviously time traveled to be on the cover of a book. Personal context made the learning relevant, important, authentic, and fun. (Even if the personal context was invented!)

One boy in the class related to me how he was trying to get to the time period of World War II in England, but a miscalculation landed him in the time period of the French Renaissance in France. With all of the matter-of-factness of someone talking about a trip to visit the local zoo, he confided that he still hoped to get to England but that learning about the Mona Lisa on the way hadn't been that bad. -Peggy

There is no one answer to improving learning, but all answers to improving learning are rooted in the experience of the student created by the context of the learning. Students (make that people) read, write, or calculate at high levels when there is a personal interest in doing so and thus the experience is authentic and personal.

I do not speak German, but I do know the word "sudbahnhof" (south rail station). I only heard the word once, and that was about 25 years ago. I have never actually used the word since. So why do I know this word so well? The context of learning counts and probably far more than we have really considered.

In this particular case I was leaving a hotel in Vienna with my two young children. The concierge assured me, in English, that the best way to the train station where we were ticketed to travel was by tram, and that we could get on right in front of the hotel. I only needed to get off at the right stop. He told me to get off when they announced "sudbahnhof." I had high motivation to learn, as I did not want to miss our train, and then there was the added emotion of feeling the responsibility for my children. And now that word is forever mine, without my intending that it be so. -Peggy

Personal interest implies that motives and emotions are in play. (Not getting lost in a foreign country with two young children in tow provides a context for a strong personal interest.) For some students, that interest is only the desire to please an adult. But only pleasing an adult has real limits and does not produce the depth of understanding that appears when the student has other and personal attachment to the learning. We seldom see this "engagement" factor included in discussions of educational practice.

Those emotions and motivations include the teacher. A teacher who has tapped into the excitement, intrigue, delight and fun of a topic cannot help but transmit this to the student. We have never seen any of these emotions happen as a student completes a worksheet of content void of context. It is a bit like filing a tax return. Most do it to avoid the penalties, but not because it brings joy. (Apologies to the tax accountants among us for whom the opposite might be true.) And they certainly do not continue to do it any longer than they must. In that respect the choice of project rests in both teacher and student because together they create the context for learning in which the motivation, and thus the learning, is high.

The right project turns out to be a natural vehicle for context that is both valuable and fun. One great example of this was the Hockey Project. It began when a first-grade teacher showed the class a short clip on force and motion in which a hockey puck was referenced. The children wanted to know more about that "puck thing." The teacher, who knew a bit about and liked hockey but could not answer all the questions from her students about the sport, suggested to the children that they find the answers together. Together they listed their questions, discussed where they might find their answers, and wrote a letter to the local hockey team to invite a representative to come to talk to them.

As is the case when interest is sparked, answers to questions led to more questions and the teacher began to imagine the possibilities for learning the curriculum with hockey as the driving topic. The teacher had no idea that the Hockey Project would continue through the whole year. It continued because new avenues for learning kept opening, the children remained curious and engaged, and the teacher had the courage to step into the unknown.

By the end of year, the class had, among other things, received a lesson on hockey from the Washington Capitals along with equipment and shirts, built a full-sized hockey rink in the gym, and written and produced a movie on hockey which was attended by a Washington Capitals' representative.

In the beginning of this book, and on the description of this book online, we were clear that this book is not a book of lesson plans. In our opinion, make that very strong opinion, if a teacher is following someone else's lesson plan then an activity is taking place, not an authentic learning experience.

Don't get us wrong, there are wonderful lesson plans out there. Sometimes lesson plans written by someone else might be a wonderful way to start to find a context that works for your students. All of our teachers have written solid lesson plans to support their projects. The difference is that they are willing to adapt, or even totally scrap a plan, if the context is not working. And if context is not working, then it is highly unlikely that ownership is happening. Even year by year, our teachers have found that previous plans are a great starting point, but they need to be adapted to meet the interests and needs of their current students.

In our own fifth-grade curriculum there is a segment on Pompeii in social studies along with some ideas for instruction and some resources. For one of our fifth-grade teachers, this already existing curriculum content has served well as the jumping off point for the development of a great authentic project because students are typically fascinated by the story of Pompeii.

The study of Pompeii in her room included the creation of a large, beautiful tile mosaic in the style of those discovered in Pompeii. Poems were written to capture the emotion of the lost lives. Models of volcanoes were built demonstrating the different types and forces of eruptions and clay castes were created to replicate the archeological finds. These are examples of taking an idea from a topic of study to an authentic project for the learners. In a third-grade classroom the teacher used a weather unit from the curriculum as the starting place for the Extreme Weather Project. There is lots of excitement to be found in the study of tornadoes, hurricanes, floods, and droughts. Students could delve into the phenomena that most intrigued them while the teacher could weave in plenty of science and math to accompany the research, writing and modeling.

All of these projects turned out to be unique, however, because the teacher was alert to the context that the students themselves pursued based on personal interest. This is what turned the activities into authentic learning experiences.

Master teachers do this with all of their lesson plans. Lesson plans are important so that teachers know what they want to accomplish, how they "hope" to accomplish it, what materials they need, etc. But a teacher who ignores the context in which the lesson is happening misses that golden opportunity to truly engage the students in front of them, and have the students internalize the objective being taught.

As we previously discussed, open-ended projects are the best way to tap into what is currently happening in the classroom. If our final goal is reaching the destination of internalization of the lesson, certainly having students so excited and engaged that they are dragging a teacher out of another classroom to view what their class has discovered, then it is mission accomplished. And if you want to see what one of the authors of this book really does look like, check out the cover of *The Mysteries of Harris Burdick*.

Chapter Six

It's a Bird, It's a Plane
No, It's Super Teaching

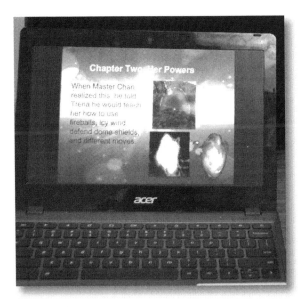

I had just started to work on this chapter when it was time to leave to listen to an astronaut speak on our local university campus. Speaking about his journey to be one of the twelve men on this planet who have walked on the moon, he continually brought up how much fun being an astronaut was. Here he was discussing the very serious, and dangerous, topic of space exploration, and you could tell he was remembering a past where he had basically had a blast. -Ellie

If you wanted to walk into a classroom that just oozed fun, the Superhero Project was the classroom to see. Superhero pictures and stories were everywhere. How can you not smile and enjoy yourself when surrounded by Batman, Spiderman, and Superwoman?

The project started after the teacher, a certified sports addict, had attempted a project about sports. Even with his enthusiasm, and with a class full of children infatuated with football, the children never totally engaged. This surprised many people, and we will admit that we can't explain why some projects "click" with certain groups of kids and some don't. But if it doesn't "click," then time to move on.

After the sports project, the teacher decided to ask the kids what interested them. He surveyed the class and then the kids voted. They wanted to do a project about superheroes. This became an avenue for writing and storyboarding, exploring the concept of identities both seen and unseen, even discovering the events in history that gave rise to the creation of superheroes like Superman. This was followed by an exploration of who our real-life heroes are, and what the qualities are that make them our "superheroes."

There is a perception problem when working in a classroom full of children who are engaged with authentic projects. When you walk into a classroom where children are truly engaged in learning through projects, everyone seems happily busy. With the perception of what a "good" classroom should look like, walking into a room where children are painting pictures of Superman and hanging Spiderman from the ceiling, a visitor may leave with the impression that there is way too much fun going on, and not enough learning.

Why is having fun considered to be most appropriate for recess, or that learning and fun are mutually exclusive? The astronaut mentioned at the beginning of this chapter was involved in one of the most demanding and dangerous careers known to mankind. And yet his presentation was engaging and totally entertaining. He made it clear that his job was fun. Perhaps the fact that he loved his job, and considered it fun, made it possible for him to achieve at a level above what most earthbound humans can only dream about. Perhaps all of the thousands of engineers and scientists behind the scenes were also having a great time at work and were willing to go that extra mile (or in this case, 230,000 plus miles) to achieve the goal of landing humans on the moon.

There is a fine, but very clear, line between having your students working on an arts and crafts activity and actually being engaged in authentic learning. As our staff first engaged in teaching through projects, it was a line we struggled to explain. We knew that we were teaching, meeting curriculum goals, and our students were achieving. However, we did note that when we walked into a classroom it did often appear that the students were engaged in arts and crafts and just having fun. We actually had to sit, watch, and observe to see if we could explain the difference.

What we found was that the teacher was very involved in listening, talking with, and directing students. As the students became more comfortable with learning this way, less redirection was required. Students using math to cut string and using measurement and angles to hang superheroes in a classroom were being guided by the teacher using the math language and skills required to complete the task.

The Colonial Feast Project had all of the elements of fun but addressed the learning in a very obvious way. At any time that you dropped into the room you would find children busily researching the time of the American Colonies, but they were also well aware that there was a feast in the offing. If a student had decided to study the life of Benjamin Franklin, that student was also wondering what Ben would have typically had for dinner and if it was a dish that could be added to the class menu.

As mentioned earlier, we have a garden, a separate project, that could provide produce and herbs to harvest for the meal. Food, the preparation of it, and the planning of the feast gave an authentic center to the learning process. And the student questions abounded. Why do onions make you cry? What plants are native to the area? How long does it take bread yeast to rise? Why does it rise? How do you know which mushrooms are edible?

Additionally, there were the logistics of pulling off a banquet with 90 fifth-graders and their teachers. Planning for success involved decisions of time and space that meant plenty of additional applied math.

One teacher decided to use students to change the bulletin board paper on several bulletin boards in a classroom. The lesson plan included objectives in perimeter, area, and measurement. What was planned to be a one-hour task turned into a week-long endeavor as the students attempted to change the paper.

These students had several years of measurement worksheets in their past, yet they had no idea how to actually apply this skill. The teacher gave them direction, and redirection, but the students needed to figure out how to accomplish the task on their own. So, years of worksheets on measurement had basically accomplished - nothing! However, after finally covering the five bulletin boards the students had truly mastered and internalized the skills required.

An adult walking into the room would have seen a pile of bulletin board paper, scissors, staplers, tape, and lots of other craft materials. You would have also seen students whispering, laughing, and having a great time. There was also the "secret" problem solving, and solution, of putting up a poster to cover a spot the students missed on one of the boards. Instead of getting more bulletin board paper, the students figured out the area needed to be covered and found the perfect poster to cover it. It was then a class inside joke for the rest of the year about not moving the poster.

Unless you stopped and listened for an extended period of time, you would not realize what learning was taking place. It may seem like a waste of time to spend a week trying to cover bulletin boards, but one could argue it is truly a waste of time to spend years on worksheets that result in no real student learning. At one point, as a group of fifth-grade students worked on a project to redesign a school closet into an office space, one boy trying to make a shelf that would fit suddenly jumped up and exclaimed, "So that's why we have fractions!"

Walking into a classroom where students are happily in the process of drawing huge superheroes on five-foot sections of paper does appear to be simple arts and crafts. But stop and listen to the discourse taking place, with the subtle guidance of the classroom teacher, and you begin to realize the powerful learning that is happening.

And if students feel that they are having fun, creating, drawing, discussing, and displaying work, all the better.

One morning I stopped by a third-grade classroom where students were finding patterns in math that would explain floor designs. One student stood beside his desk bouncing up and down and humming to himself happily, as he simultaneously wrote out a pattern. I leaned down to ask him what he was doing and he excitedly whispered to me that he had just discovered a pattern that "no one else in the world" yet knew about, adding "don't tell anybody!" The secret appeared to be that not only had he discovered a new pattern, but instead of working on boring math problems, he was having fun. That incident reminded me of how very often a student will tell me, as if sharing a well-kept secret, "we're having a lot of fun in our class today!" -Peggy

Chapter Seven

Failure Is Not an Option
(But It Should Be)

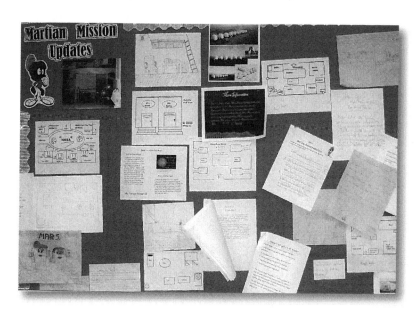

Two of the teachers from our school had an extraordinary opportunity a few summers ago. The two teachers, along with 18 others nationally, were selected by NASA to fly out to the John Glenn Research Center in Ohio to work for a week with NASA scientists. One of the first things the teachers learned about was how NASA classifies missions. A "C" mission was allowed to fail. A "B" mission should succeed, but failure was a possibility. An "A" mission must succeed.

When the teachers began a new Martian Colony Project the following fall they discussed this mission criteria with their fifth-graders. The students were able to give examples of what they thought would fit into each mission category. They were able to, on their own, figure out that an "A" mission involved astronauts, which is why failure was not an option. When an "A" mission failed, astronauts died. They also developed an understanding of why it was okay for a "C" mission to fail. NASA scientists learned from their failures.

When children work on authentic projects, these projects need to be considered "C" missions. Teachers need to allow students to "fail" and to learn from these "failures." Whenever an adult hits a roadblock in life, everyone jumps on board the "learn from your failures" bandwagon. "It's ok to fail." "If you aren't willing to risk failure, you can't succeed." However, we seem to forget this when teaching children. With children, it seems that the only acceptable outcome is perfection. Perfect projects, displayed on perfect bulletin boards, with perfect "A"s displayed on each perfect paper. We lose sight of the fact that it is the journey to excellence, with many corrections along the way, that we need to focus on in order to improve learning.

One of the main reasons educators do not jump on board the authentic learning bandwagon is that fear of student failure. Using projects to teach in a classroom involves a pretty big leap of faith. Teachers are moving away from presenting the cookie cutter lessons that are being presented in every classroom. Sometimes, these are lessons that have been structured by their school district to promote student success on standardized tests.

What also adds to this risk is that true authentic learning demands that the teacher take a novel stance. Like other standard teaching approaches, it starts with a teacher prompt and has guidelines based on what the teacher hopes to accomplish. It is also based on school district curriculum. However, it is essential that it be student directed and led. Talk about risking a "failure mission!" But if we look at what we really want to accomplish with students - increasing their ability to read, write, calculate, and be critical thinkers - then we can go back to the NASA criteria where "C" missions are acceptable as students learn from their "failures."

As we queried in chapter two, how do students direct and lead in authentic learning? We looked at this, discussed this, observed teachers in our building during instruction, and discovered another common thread for the teachers having the most success with authentic learning. They were listening to their students and willing to let failure as well as success be a learning opportunity. That means that after the teachers introduced the topic to the class, they listened for what the students wished to know, found intriguing, and claimed as the area that they would take on. Then the teachers guided their students to what they needed to research, create, and present in order to accomplish their own goals. And if the chosen direction did not work, the only failure was in not seeking an alternative direction.

Over the course of several years of the fifth-grade class designing and creating a Martian Colony, the students of each class took directions unique to their own interests. Different students created and ran a Martian government, focused on health care, developed a cattle ranch as a food source, built a Martian lander and rover, and fielded several sports teams representing their colony. In each case, potential failure was a launching pad for learning.

One student, an elected member of the Martian government, wanted to pass a law that every pod must have a security system installed. She also wanted to own and operate the only security company in the colony. The other children serving on the Martian government innately knew that this presented a conflict of interest. They also questioned whether it was good to have only one company as a supplier of a service. Couldn't the owner charge unreasonable prices? Would service be good with no competition? All questions were asked somewhat calmly and with a fair amount of respect. (As mentioned earlier, the colony was "real" to these students, so sometimes discussions became animated.)

This led to research by the students on government laws, promoting self-interests, and monopolies. The security system proponent internalized some of the concerns, and eventually agreed that there could not be a law requiring a security system in each pod. She did explain, however, that in a new colony, there were many businesses without competition, this was just good business, offering a unique and needed service. (We definitely expect to see this young lady as owner and CEO of a major corporation some day!)

The students designing a Martian cattle ranch did not realize they were going to encounter a significant financial problem. They found out well into their research that, based on the cost per pound of sending something to Mars, the cows they planned on launching from Earth to eventually eat on Mars would, in the end, cost thousands of dollars per half pound hamburger.

This was not a surprise to the teachers. As the students became more engaged in planning for their ranch, the teachers realized that the students were going to encounter several major problems, including cost. The students were engaged, researching, designing, writing, and calculating with great enthusiasm. There was no reason for the teachers to shut this down.

At the appropriate point, the teachers interjected cost analysis into this project. (Unlike the security system concerns, which were caught quickly by classmates, the Martian ranch proposals and planning went on for several months before the teachers felt it was time for some redirection.) This was presented as a non-judgmental math lesson.

During the course of this lesson, the students realized they had a problem. Their initial reaction was to shut the ranch down. The teachers agreed there was a problem, but also reminded the students that planning for a food supply in the colony was extremely important. The students were encouraged to continue their research to find a solution to this problem. The students solved this problem by deciding to change their ranch to a farm (researching and explaining the difference to classmates). The final decision was to only bring dairy animals and to use them for dairy products.

Even if the students had not been able to solve their financial problem, their planning to that point had moved them along not only in their understanding of Mars and the problems of colonization, but in their basic fifth-grade academic skills.

It is also important to remember that students are not going to come up with solutions for problems that adults would. Bringing dairy cows to Mars may not be a practical solution in the end. However, for fifth-graders, the solution used the kind of higher level thinking skills that we want to encourage.

NASA certainly recognized the value of the fifth-grade work when they invited the two fifth-grade teachers to the NASA Glenn summer program. (Most of the teachers invited were high school teachers. Not because NASA was looking for high school teachers, NASA was not receiving reports on projects involving higher level and creative thinking from elementary schools. Why not?)

As the staff and students became more comfortable with risking failure we began to see the demise of the traditional displays of student work where all looked the same, full of perfect work created by perfect students. Instead, we saw diverse displays full of student work in progress. Few of the displayed pieces were perfect. The information presented varied widely around the main project topic. And the work itself improved over time as the learning progressed.

This acceptance of failure as important to learning was again evidenced one day during the visit of two outside administrators. They were amazed to see fifth-grade students working so independently. The students were on task, engaged, and eager to share what they were working on with the visitors. When asked a question about her project, one student could not answer. In a traditional classroom environment, that would have been the endpoint of the interaction, with the student's lack of response viewed as "failure."

As the two adults moved on, the student pulled out her tablet and looked up the answer. She then located the two adults further down the hall and politely informed them that she now had the answer to their question. This young lady had ownership of her project and saw "not knowing" not as failure, but as an opportunity for learning.

For teachers to be willing to allow students to experience "failures," the support and encouragement of the building administrators is necessary. At present and for the past many years, the success of the building principal has been judged by the standardized state test scores of the school. Even though our test scores were rising as we compared growth over the course of a year, these tests measure only a narrow band of knowledge, a band far too narrow to prepare students for their future in a quickly changing world.

Administrators need to be able to support, explain, and encourage both their own teachers and others who interact with their staff about how important and fundamental to student success the authentic process is. Authentic learning taps into skills and higher order thinking of an entirely different order and assumes the long view in building those abilities. Valuing those higher abilities will open the door to the use of better strategies for teaching and learning, such as the use of authentic projects, and an acknowledgement of the need for the "C" mission.

Initially, we also struggled with how to grade work when failure was not only allowed, but sometimes encouraged. We realized that "failed" projects needed to be graded on the strength of the academics involved, not whether or not the idea actually worked in the end. (The students designing the ranch on Mars all received high grades as their work was comprehensive and academically above grade level in reading, writing, and math.)

For true and successful authentic learning, teachers need to listen to their students, let them lead the project, and allow for those "C" missions to occur. And administrators need to support these "C" missions as well.

As we wrapped up this chapter, Space X made the first test flight of "Falcon Heavy," the largest rocket currently in production on Earth. The owner of Space X, Elon Musk, had an interesting payload on board - his own Tesla automobile. He made it clear that there was a good chance the new technology used in "Falcon Heavy" might explode on the launch pad.

Watching the 6,000 employees of Space X view the launch, you didn't see scientists and engineers in fear of losing their jobs. What you saw was laughing, cheering, yelling, and excitement. No matter what happened, these people were thrilled. It was a perfect launch. The pictures of "Starman" sitting in the Tesla as it sped through space were amazing. ("C" Mission - "Starman" was an empty space suit, but man, did he look cool!) The twin rocket boosters and central core detached perfectly and headed back towards a landing on Earth for refurbishment and reuse.

The twin rocket boosters made an amazing and perfect landing in Florida. However, the central core did not land successfully on the recovery ship at sea. It actually damaged the drone ship before it crashed into the ocean.

Every headline we read after the launch declared the mission a huge success. And it was. However, you can bet that the next day, engineers were poring over the data from the central tank "failure" to find out what went wrong. They will learn from this "failure." Let's give our kids the same opportunity.

Chapter Eight

Quiet, Please,
The Show Is About to Begin

In a totally random conversation with a visiting friend, I found out that her high school daughter and a friend had approached the principal in a school in our district about developing a curriculum for entrepreneurship and marketing. Not only did the young lady and her friend develop this curriculum, they taught it this past year at their high school. In a half-hour conversation with her mother, I heard enough to write another book.

One huge takeaway was the anecdote that her mother told me about the first day of class. The students in the class were fooling around, not paying attention, and not listening to the lesson presented by the two seniors. The next day things went much better. Why? Because the two student-instructors got the students involved in creating their own projects on the second day of class. The young lady reported back to her mother that just standing in front of a class lecturing was not going to work. She figured this out in one day. Behavior problems solved. -Ellie

You never know what to expect when you walk into one of our classrooms. Ice hockey rinks, gladiators in full dress, a court in session, a meeting of the United Nations, Mission Control...

Walking into a "Rent Party" set during the Harlem Renaissance is certainly not what you would expect to find in a twenty-first century elementary school classroom. But, maybe you should. This student written, produced, directed and performed production not only reinforced curriculum concepts and academic content, but also taught those in the audience about the history of the rent parties in Harlem.

The "Rent Party" was an outgrowth of the Harlem Renaissance Project, a project developed by one of our teachers. This project encompassed a period of history that this teacher had spent much time exploring out of personal interest. When she discovered that her interest was shared by her students, they designed a project together. One of their decisions was to share their learning through a play.

Does this sound like the Opera Project? In many respects they were similar. And both revolved around topics the teachers were interested in, the performing arts for one teacher, and the Harlem Renaissance for the other. This is where the fun comes in for the teacher. (We have already established that fun at school is a good thing.) If you are going to pour your heart and soul into a project, it should be something you enjoy. Something you are really interested in. It should be fun. And a by-product of fun is engagement. And a by-product of engagement is better behaved students.

With the Opera Project and the Harlem Renaissance Project, the teachers picked a medium in which they were interested. Both had a great deal of background knowledge. Both already had many of the materials that they would need. The teachers were engaged and enthusiastic. They didn't mind spending the weekend thinking about their project because they already did that before their passion even became a project. (You have probably already figured out that one of the authors of this book is infatuated with the study of space. As in one of us took her first teaching job in Houston so she could date NASA scientists. She ended up marrying one, and he was hugely helpful with the Martian Colony Project, as were the two Trekkers they raised.)

We pursued teaching through projects principally because we believed that it increased learning for all students and most especially for those groups of children who traditionally struggled. In our school, these groups include those living in poverty, those in the process of learning English, and those identified as needing special education. By increasing the engagement of students in the learning process, by honoring the role of the learner's interests, and by creating a context for the learning, we have watched our children grow. And we have watched their behavior dramatically improve.

The teacher excitement and engagement, which led to student excitement and engagement, was responsible for this remarkable improvement in behavior school-wide. If you tire of managing behavior issues in the classroom, we strongly suggest that you think about authentic projects.

Controlling a classroom full of children who are creating a stage production, and the classroom management involved, might be enough to make a teacher run for cover. It certainly seems to make sense that it would be easier to control a classroom full of children sitting in desks in neat rows than to control a room (with children spilling out into the hallway for more space) of children working on ten different things at the same time.

However, this is not what we found. Teaching using authentic projects caused behavior problems across the school to drop dramatically. This was not a slight change, this was a dramatic 80% change. (We kept track of the numbers and have binders full of data.) It is not hard to understand why this would happen. The children wanted to be in the classroom because they found it interesting to be there. They found it engaging. They found it fun.

But there were other and less obvious realities that supported better and more productive behavior. In traditional classroom experiences, the student is frequently in the audience during much of the school day. Learning through authentic projects, the student experience is seldom that of being in an audience, but rather as the captain of his or her own ship.

Because the projects meant working with others, there was a constant social context. Additionally, and perhaps most importantly, the student relationship with the teacher became one in which the student felt that the teacher really knew him or her as an individual. In fact, the teachers *did* know their students better and could better respond to their differing needs.

A common fear of teachers who have not tried to do a project is that the room will dissolve into chaos because the teacher will not be able to control the room. And if the teacher is not prepared, that could indeed happen, but that would happen to an unprepared teacher no matter what the approach to instruction. When students are working on something where they have ownership and interest, they are not out of control because their behaviors are directed toward the project.

When the teacher is not expending energy just controlling the learning environment, that teacher can devote time to responding to student ideas and questions as they arise. Good, authentic projects involve such high levels of student engagement that discipline issues that arise from the student who feels unvalued or bored drop away.

Before embarking on authentic teaching through projects, we had more than one staff meeting devoted to how we should best handle behavior problems. Typically, these meetings ended up in a general frustration that there was no one magic answer and that the "office" needed to just "fix" those students by, presumably, frightening them into obedience as needed.

After five years of working towards having projects dominate the learning environment, we again held a staff meeting to discuss student behavior. It began with a discussion of the importance of building good relationships with the students, a tactic that had been floated before, but this time there was strong agreement that this could indeed happen in the classroom and that the creation of that relationship is a major benefit of working with projects.

When discussion turned to the student with exceptional issues, teachers freely offered strategies that they had found helped them to reach those children. Addressing those exceptional children in a room where behavior is so generally positive was a far less overwhelming task for the teacher. Teachers spoke of delving into the students' backgrounds to better understand the student, they spoke of finding a way to build the all-important relationship, of varying the approach to content - and no one spoke of the need for punishment as a solution.

Our beliefs about projects and behavior were put to the test one year when our fourth grade received 12 new boys from various places in the course of two months, all of whom were moving in from outside the school district as a result of being removed from their previous homes due to drug use and general neglect. All were gravely behind academically, one was completely illiterate at the age of ten, and all had learned to survive by striking out first and often.

We already had children in fourth grade with difficult home issues, but with whom we had, over time, been able to build productive relationships. However, those children, already vulnerable, were often the first to be attacked by the new arrivals and thus were becoming unable to focus in the classroom. There were four classrooms in fourth grade, and the number of issues in each room was now too high.

Our response to the problem was multifaceted and involved one-on-one mentoring, support beyond the school day, and counseling groups for anger management. But the one factor that made these supports work was that the students, regardless of the situation of each, wanted to be in the classroom and be part of what was happening there. Their cooperation in addressing their problems was motivated by the classroom projects.

When our students first started to visit the final products or presentations from class projects, there was concern about the behavior of the students not only attending these events, but also of the students participating. And initially this was a valid concern. As the students gained experience with projects, they also began to appreciate others' projects. Not only did we see improved behavior for those attending the presentations, we also saw improved behavior from the presenters.

Rarely were the presenters sitting for long time periods waiting to present their projects. The nature of the projects themselves led to a much more interactive and dynamic presentation. Due to the multi-tiered aspects of projects, students were able to present on their level and truly understand and engage in what they were presenting. This, in turn, truly engaged the audience attending the presentation.

Tours of the Martian Colony included scheduling and rotation of presenters and tour guides, colony "future-actors," behind the scenes technology managers, and colony inspectors/repair-persons. (The colony was built totally out of boxes, tape, and glue, and required frequent inspection and repair. You certainly would not want a breach of the walls, resulting in a loss of breathable atmosphere. As we stated before, the colony was "real" to the fifth-graders.)

As tours of the Martian Colony were interactive and involved many stations for "guests" to visit, the teachers were also able to schedule "high energy" tour guides into positions that channeled their energy productively. Students could also be placed in areas with close adult supervision if needed. Scheduling was done as another layer to guarantee student success in their roles in the colony presentation. Success breeds self-esteem, which in turn leads to better behavior.

These opportunities for diverse and scaffolded presentation were readily available and tended to develop along with the project as it unfolded. The two students who became the car lot managers had in the course of the project developed their own roles based on their interests and were eagerly and actively involved in the presentation of the car lot. In the past, both of these students had struggled during traditional presentations of traditional products.

The student written, produced, directed, and performed Rent Parties had the same effect. The students had ownership of and context with their work. They were engaged. This in turn engaged the audience. While addressing curriculum content in social studies, reading, written language, and even math (with set construction), these vignettes had the added benefit of introducing both the students involved and the audience to a part of American history that many had not heard of before.

The classroom teacher's passion became the students' passion, which in turn engaged the audience. Learning was achieved and internalized. And behavior was not an issue.

Chapter Nine

Light My Fire

I taught for years using a very solid, research-based reading program developed for significantly below grade level readers. The books in the program were high interest and engaged my students. I believed in this program, I enjoyed using it, and it worked - for awhile.

After several years using this program, I found myself going into autopilot. I had read each book so many times that I couldn't remember what I had already discussed with the students, what I had taught, or what they had responded to. Even taking lengthy notes, I couldn't separate out previous years from the current year in my head. The spontaneity and engagement of my teaching was gone, and student achievement suffered. This was an expensive reading program, purchased for three different grade levels. Our school was literally heavily invested in this program, and I had totally burned out on it. -Ellie

While discussing all of the successes we have had with student achievement using authentic projects, we have also frequently mentioned teacher engagement. It is difficult to impossible to decouple student achievement from teacher engagement and enthusiasm. It is an extremely rare learner who can maintain engagement and enthusiasm for learning with a disengaged teacher.

The teaching profession has changed considerably over the last few decades and burnout is at an all-time high. Who can blame a teacher for burning out when faced with the expectations and pressures put on a teacher today? And yet, the fires of creativity are what make learning rigorous.

I observed one teacher's loss of enthusiasm without being able to pinpoint what was going on with her. One thing I knew for certain was that she was a creative, as well as a competent, teacher. We were in year two of experimenting with authentic projects. I asked her to meet with me and simply asked if she would be willing to be a leader in exploring the introduction of authentic projects. She took it on without hesitation. And no surprise, her enthusiasm improved. The spark was back. -Peggy

The story of this teacher exemplifies the difference between the engaged and the unengaged teacher. This teacher had come to teach at our school right out of college. She was conscientious and hardworking from the beginning and carried through with all district requirements in a timely and efficient way. Additionally, she truly loved working with children.

Initially, her teaching reflected what her grade level team members worked on together and she was often the one who made copies for all of the team members of the student work that they chose. She was naturally collaborative.

Over a period of the next five years she continued to reliably cover the curriculum, but she was less than excited about what she was doing. A naturally energetic person, she filled the need to feel efficacy through involvement in activities outside of the school.

After her meeting with administration, she began having frequent chats with our "opera lady" (the teacher with the Opera Project). Together they explored what successful authentic teaching, authentic learning, and authentic projects need. This previously disengaged teacher was the one who ended up creating one of our most engaging projects. She had no intention of having the project go on for an entire year, but as she gained skill in incorporating curriculum and searched actively for approaches that her students could be excited about, the possibilities just kept opening up, especially with math. And she began to arrive to school each morning already excited about what that day's journey could be. And so did her students.

As the teachers in our building engaged in authentic learning, we noticed another positive by product. In today's world, when one is bored, the default move is a reach for the cell phone. Cell phones today have hugely and dramatically changed our daily lives and there are many positive aspects to everyone basically having a personal computer in their pocket. But cell phones have a time and place.

No one would suggest that a teacher should be engaged on a cell phone while teaching. Cell phones have an addictive aspect, and it is hard to keep that phone in your pocket without checking that one text, email, or posting on Facebook. Nothing sends a message quicker to a child that you are not interested in what they are doing than spending time on Facebook instead of focusing on the child.

At first, we tried limiting the use of cell phones in the classroom, but as they became more technologically advanced, and our authentic projects became more technologically advanced, they reappeared as a support to student work. What we noticed, however, was that as the teachers became re-engaged and enthused about what they were teaching, the cell phones truly became a tool to support work in the classroom, not a way to "kill time" as a bored teacher caught up on Facebook postings in order to stay awake while students completed a worksheet for drilling facts out of context.

As we have stated, teachers frequently picked projects of interest to them. Even if through student discourse the project veered down an unexpected path, the basic underlying project was something the teacher enjoyed.

A teacher who cares nothing about Pro Football would not have much success with an authentic project about the NFL. However, take an Opera Project, and through student discourse, you could end up with an opera about a Super Bowl victory, or loss. As the students move the opera in a new direction, the teacher is learning and engaged. And thus, you avoid the pitfalls of the boredom that sets in from teaching the same thing over and over again.

As authentic learning is student led, these new directions every year mean that the projects do not get stale for the teacher or the student. Current events can and should shape projects. This can be on a national level for older students, and on a local and personal level for all students. Through projects, events causing concern and even stress for children and adults can be addressed in a context appropriate for the age group involved.

Living in the suburbs of Washington, D.C., the children at our school are constantly bombarded with news about the federal government on both a national, local, and personal level. As many, if not most, of our parents have jobs that are somehow tied into the government, this increases our student awareness, and often stress. Events such as government shutdowns directly impact our students, and many of our staff who have spouses with government dependent jobs. Government employees on furlough are not buying coffee at Starbucks on the way to work or shopping for non-essentials after work, so the impact trickles down quickly to all areas of the economy.

As the national government is just that - national - events in Congress impact all children and adults across the nation in one way or another. Regardless of where you teach, we are all living in a complicated, stressful world. Add the stress of working with stressed out families, on top of what a teacher is already responsible for, and teacher burnout makes even more sense.

Many of our projects have had a component that has been tied into the government or economy. We have been led to this by student discourse. Student work has addressed these issues and concerns through creative writing, charity fundraising, and in many cases the study of how government works through the creation of student governments, courts, and legislation. And while this doesn't solve the stress that our children (and adults) are under, it certainly doesn't hurt to have an outlet to delve into these topics in a supervised, educational setting.

We also found that as authentic projects dug deeper than traditional learning, the teachers themselves were constantly understanding and learning new things. Even listening to diverse student views on topics caused self-reflection and growth for many of our staff members. Again, no tedium there.

The teacher's own creativity and attention to student discourse meant that there were continually new paths to explore. So, the repetitious, straight path, traveled year after year into monotony, became a winding, curving path, with new surprises at every turn. The journey was anything but boring!

Chapter Ten

May We Present

I have frequently, over my many years in schools, sat through a classroom presentation where one student after another got up and mumbled his or her way through a list of facts. The teacher usually had to make continual reminders to the class to be quiet and pay attention while, as for me, I wanted to poke my eyes out after about the fourth speaker. -Peggy

Traditional presentations of student projects involve students holding up and reading from a tri-board. Tri-boards are not, in themselves, a poor way to represent learning. They become poor when teachers hand out a grading rubric which demands that the title be in the same spot followed by a "cookie cutter" introduction, three pictures with captions, etc. Certainly, have your parents type it all up for you if your keyboarding skills are lacking or your handwriting is poor. As a matter of fact, just have your parents complete the project for you. Then you can stand in front of the class and read what your parents wrote. It will look better, sound better (actually, not really), be easier to correct, and then the teacher can give you a good grade.

So as educators, we take what may have been a strong learning journey, with academic and emotional growth, and grade the entire thing on whether or not it looks like the teacher's model and follows the classroom example. That is not to say that we shouldn't model, teach and encourage that there should be certain elements in a final presentation. In fact, we should definitely model and teach these things. But in the final process, we need to be careful that we don't shut down all the creativity and personal learning that has taken place by demanding conformity over good content in a final product.

Aside from the Opera Project's production, most of our projects have at first used tri-boards full of information as the exhibition artifact. As a school, we quickly moved past the "cookie cutter" tri-board. This can only take place in a school where administration understands and accepts what our final goal is, as these tri-boards frequently contained errors.

Students will exhibit the most growth when the teacher points out some key or repetitive mistakes in student work and works with the students to correct these. In this collaboration between teacher and student, learning is internalized and growth occurs. For some students, this will result in a very polished product. For others, especially struggling students, the correction of a few key errors may leave a product with many mistakes still in place. But again, learning has been internalized and growth has occurred. The tri-boards, or other products, were truly done by children with developing skills and this allowed us to acknowledge these developing skills. And the products were wonderful.

As we got further down the road in our project skills, we began to recognize that how the learning is shared in the end was a field of opportunity for learning all of its own. Most curriculums have the ubiquitous objective of writing a persuasive letter. That is the closest we come to thinking about convincing others through the power of our words. Projects at our school concluded with an exhibition of the work to which parents, classmates, and community members were invited. The exhibition of the work was a powerful opportunity to closely consider how we engage and convince others of our thoughts.

No one knows better than students what they would like to have happen when attending a presentation, and it is not to sit through an endless recitation of scripted facts. Part of authentic teaching is to involve the students in what, when, and how they will share what they are doing with others. It turns out that this has more possibilities than any one person can come up with.

A recent invitation arrived in the office to invite staff to attend Amazing Adventure Stories. In this project, each student wrote an adventure story with a setting, character, and style of choice. This took place after a review of the folklore and legends of different countries and cultures. Each student then decided how to share their story.

Time in class had been devoted to considering how best each student could communicate his or her story to an audience. They tried out the presentations on each other and solicited feedback. And then they polished the final project into a "must see." When it came time to share the stories, the students had to spread out over three rooms in order to accommodate everything from an animated slideshow on a screen to a diorama, interactive screenshots on tablets, and a telling of the story by a "storyteller" in full costume.

The project called "The Lie" stood on its own as a performance of students' poetry long before it was captured in video and shared more widely. This project started when the classroom teacher realized that, in the course of studying cultures of the world, her students needed an outlet to share their feelings about their unique multicultural and multiracial backgrounds.

"The Lie" was first presented live in a classroom in our building. The words were personal and passionate and you could have heard a pin drop in the room even though it was generally packed tight with five through eleven-year-olds. Teachers and other adults in the building returned to see several presentations of the performance whenever their schedules allowed, entranced by the power of the students' words. When this happens, the learning is not only that of the presenting student but also of the attending audience.

As we have discussed previously, the Martian Colony Project ended with a guided tour of the colony. The first year this was simply a presentation of the colony bulletin board. The second year included the board with the colony design on it and the student constructed Prototype Pod. The third year the students added a class constructed rover full of science experiments designed by the students. These experiments were represented in a Martian Virtual Science Fair. The experiments were proposed, designed, and represented by the rover model constructions, following the scientific process. (A teacher favorite was the photograph of the exploded soda can in the student's home freezer, representing the outcome of taking a canned soda onto the freezing surface of Mars. The teachers were wondering if they needed to hide from that parent when she showed up to tour the colony.)

Year by year, more was added to the colony. When an empty classroom was available one year, the class "reverse-terraformed" the entire classroom into Mars. A colony classroom was constructed, and students frequently attended class in that cramped student designed and built structure. The class was even short desks, as they were requested from Earth in September, but it takes about nine months for supplies to travel from Earth to Mars. This was explained to visitors during the tour, who delighted that several "student actors" were sitting on the floor during the presentation of the classroom. (The needed desks arrived on the last day of school, nine months to the day after being requested. This was much to the delight of the three boys who sat on the floor whenever the class worked in the Martian classroom, for the entire year!)

The final colony presentation, and all of the structures designed, built, and presented, did not evolve in one year. The teacher involved with the Opera Project made it very clear that what was being presented was also the culmination of many years of work. Some projects serendipitously became huge the first year. Others developed over many years. Some were presented after a few weeks. Others continued for the entire school year with an end of year presentation.

Teachers should not be intimidated about starting an authentic learning experience by thinking that it needs to culminate in a huge stage production, a professionally taped video, or a trip to Mars! We have seen as much engagement, growth, and enthusiasm happen with a culminating tri-board presentation. The key is that the work is shared proudly to an audience, and that the work and its presentation really belongs to the student.

Chapter Eleven

The Proof Is in the Pudding

Ingredients for an Authentic Learning Experience:

Ownership

Early foundation

Real-world application

Deliberate incorporation of student interest

Openness to the unplanned learning opportunity

Integration of content

Active learning

Valuing student inquiry

Learning from failure

Engagement

These are the ingredients that are needed for authentic teaching and authentic learning. If our goal is to educate children to thrive in a future world that we can't even comprehend, then we need to do some real "outside of the box" thinking about how we approach education. Obviously, we feel very strongly that teaching using authentic projects accomplishes this goal. Just looking at the list of "ingredients" gives one a gut feeling that "this is how you reach kids."

But a "gut feeling" is not hard data. In taking this approach to education, a huge shift from many current education practices, it would be nice to have some data to show that this approach works.

There is a national problem in education with finding a way to neatly test for what we want to accomplish with our students. We are educating children for a future that we can't predict or even comprehend, yet we are trying to evaluate them by using tests that were written to measure competence in reading, writing, and math, by filling out forms that only credit thinking "inside the box." One correct answer is not going to make it in the coming decades, yet the current way we assess is looking for just that.

Accountability is necessary, I understand that, but one encounter with another professional at a previous school I worked at left me so shaken that I feel a need to share it. It happened many years ago but impacted me so profoundly that I have never forgotten it.

While teaching a reading group, this person walked up to me and told me that I was wasting my time modeling complete sentences for the children I was working with. The current student achievement test our state was using was graded by computer, and the computer was programmed to pick out and reward the use of key words and phrases. So, according to this professional peer, I was wasting valuable time teaching the children to write using complete sentences.

This exchange horrified me. I was honestly totally astounded. Here I sat with a group of high risk, struggling children, teaching them a basic writing tool, actually THE basic writing tool. I was literally shaking. If our charge as educators is to prepare students to thrive in the future as adults, these kids better know how to formulate a sentence. A complete sentence! (I know, that is not a complete sentence, but I would have achieved a high score on the standardized assessment in use at the time.)

In defense of this peer, teachers were, and still are, under tremendous pressure to produce solid and improved test scores. However, as we mentioned above, it is difficult to impossible to find a measure for what we want to accomplish with children today. This "teaching to the test" to achieve higher test scores can be dangerous if, combined with pressure and misinterpretation, we lose sight of what is important in the classroom.

I will close this anecdote, one of the most chilling episodes from my experiences as a teacher, with the statement that I did not take the advice of this peer. -Ellie

Another, and more difficult, problem with using present tests to judge learning is that looking at the average scores in reading and math, and sometimes science, and comparing them year to year (which is the present practice nationwide for determining progress) can only be useful in determining progress if we assume that there are no changing variables to consider. Any teacher can tell you that there can be vast differences in the students in a class from one year to the next. Specifically, an increase or decrease in the number of students who speak English, who have learning disabilities, who have experienced childhood trauma, or who have serious home dysfunction. This is not only possible in many classrooms, but likely. For us, high mobility was probably the variable with the largest impact.

However, we wanted to have some window into the results of learning through authentic projects beyond the anecdotal that we have shared in this book. Therefore, we used an available standardized district test to assess reading level and math level at the beginning of the school year and again at the end of the school year for each child. We then took the difference in scores as a "growth" score and calculated an average growth by class and by grade for each year.

By doing this, we could see that each year that we used authentic projects, the average student growth increased. We could also see that this held true for both struggling students and gifted students. This trend held over the five-year period that we were measuring.

But like we said earlier, our real proof of achievement could be found in the children's expressive ability in both writing and speech, the confidence with which they approached solving problems, and the high levels of application that they willingly took on.

When researching topics for their own projects they would go above their reading level because they had discovered that those were the readings that had more information. They would persevere in a challenge, having found their own strengths as problem solvers. They would generate questions and seek the answers as an everyday practice. None of this is measurable on a standard test - and all of this is necessary to success in and out of school and over the course of a lifetime.

Chapter Twelve

OneSchoolsJourney@gmail.com

After writing a book about all of the positive reasons that schools should use authentic projects to educate their students, we feel we should discuss some of the problems we have not totally solved yet. Throughout the book, we have mentioned most, if not all, of the problems that we will bring up in this chapter. We have also previously addressed ways that we solved most of these problems in our school. However, some of our solutions were piecemeal, and some were band-aids, while we strive to come up with a better way to solve these problems.

Starting down the road to authentic learning with a teaching staff that had been trained and experienced in an instructional program with a bias toward direct teacher-led instruction was a bumpy journey. Authentic teaching requires not only a new paradigm but also that the teacher develop such habits as a focus on the student role in learning and the fostering of creative problem solving. Just as importantly, most teachers themselves have had years of schooling that did not look like authentic learning.

Ideally, teachers work in an environment where they productively support each other in learning about and developing authentic teaching opportunities. Authentic projects require both massive front loading of the process and an openness to new directions that may appear along the way. Not all teachers will be open to this process.

Collaboration with peers improves the quality through combined knowledge and ideas. However, teachers who have worked chiefly in isolation can find this step to be uncomfortable at first. We took steps to try to improve our ability to make this happen by consciously examining how we interacted. There is never a guarantee that all teachers will interact with equal ease, but focusing on what we could accomplish with children took conversation from isolated personal trials to professional collaboration.

So how do teachers support each other when they are working on different projects that are student directed in every classroom? What do teachers do who are used to sharing only worksheets, tests, homework assignments, and other materials? Many of these teachers are already feeling overloaded, overworked, and overwhelmed with expectations.

What we found was that teachers were most successful when they picked projects that deeply interested them. Their projects were a labor of love. They often already had many of the materials that they needed. And once students took the lead in the direction of the project, the students started to bring in materials from home. The teacher's role became that of facilitator and director. There was not a need for worksheets to be created. The students read and wrote as they created their own materials. They created their own math problems and solved them.

But for some teachers, even adding a "labor of love" is too much if they are already feeling that they can't handle one more thing. We can sing the praises of authentic teaching until our voices are hoarse, but if that teacher is at that tipping point, our song will not matter.

Again, not all teachers were as readily able to let go of the traditional way of instruction. And as teachers did move to authentic teaching, we had teachers at every level of experience and comfort with the process. Some teachers have a passion (very few people don't) but have not yet been able to translate that into authentic teaching in the classroom.

A big problem we faced with using authentic projects to teach was our own district report card. The report card calls for certain objectives to be taught at specific times in the year. This timeline did not always match up with the projects. For example, teaching area and perimeter might show up on the fifth-grade fall report card while it fit in perfectly during the winter when the class was designing and building the Martian Prototype Pod.

Some of the teachers solved this problem by creating an isolated "introduction" lesson when the objective needed to be taught and then returning to reinforce the objective authentically when it fit in the project. It solved the problem; however, it was a return to a teaching practice that did not have the best results with the students. Definitely a band-aid solution.

Incorporating projects into our district curriculum was also problematic at times. Even if we adjusted the time frame to match the report card, our curriculum is large and comprehensive. You really don't have a moment to spare. So how do you cover everything in the curriculum plus what you want to cover in your project? We were able to solve some of this problem with some creativity. A third-grade curriculum unit on poetry was easily adapted to writing poetry about cars as advertisements for the car lot. But this did not always work, and the problem became exacerbated when working with open-ended projects that followed student interest and need.

Another problem we encountered was the perception of what was actually happening in the classroom. Projects involve lots of hands-on planning and construction. To someone doing a quick visit, what they may see is lots of arts and crafts. Students are going home and telling their parents they spent the day gluing, cutting, and painting. This is not what parents expect to hear their children say. Even an experienced, trained educator may be surprised to walk into a classroom full of children doing what looks like arts and crafts. This can also cause concern for other supervisors who are walking into classrooms and seeing only a quick snapshot of what is going on. And if you don't stop, spend some time, and listen to what is going on, then that is what you will see.

Add to this list of perceived problems the fact that the same exact thing is not going on in every classroom. Parents often talk to other parents and can become concerned if their child is studying space while another child in the same grade is learning about ecosystems. Both children are covering the grade level curriculum, but in very different ways. (This is difficult enough with neighbors, add twins in different classrooms in the same grade and you really add to the confusion of the parent.) With time and the building of understanding with our parents, this has greatly improved over the years.

In a previous chapter, we explored our use of a final presentation to bring the parents and others outside of the classroom into a final product that demonstrated the learning that took place. We also found that having a mid-point presentation eased some of the concerns about what was going on in the classroom without waiting until the very end when perceptions were more difficult to change. We experienced much success with this, but we were not able to get every parent, or outside supervisor, in to see the final product.

Projects will be difficult to impossible without administrative support. It is one thing to have an outside supervisor walk in and question what you are doing. It is another to have your building administrator not be on board. Teaching using authentic projects is a major mindset change, and what is going on in the classroom does not look like what happens in a traditional classroom. It would be extremely difficult to switch to an authentic teaching model without administrative support. The administrators we invited to visit our classrooms left enthusiastic and very interested. We knew we were on to something good, but the outside reaction was beyond what we had imagined. That was a fantastic experience for our staff, but how does one teacher, alone in a building, bring administrators and staff on board to teaching this way?

As an administrator, I worried initially about having my staff use authentic projects knowing that if they then decided to go to teach at a different school in the future that the expectations for instruction would be very different. I did not want to diminish the professional prospects of excellent educators. In the end, though, it seems to me that a teacher who can effectively implement authentic projects has a skill set that makes them stronger teachers, regardless of a particular school's curriculum or instructional approach, because of the increased teacher awareness of the student learning experience. - Peggy

Authentic teaching works. Our belief is that it is the best way to educate this generation for the future that they will face. That doesn't mean that it is seamless. With any new approach to teaching there are bumps to be ironed out. (Or in this case, an old way of teaching that is being looked at again, as authentic projects, in many ways, resemble apprenticeships of the past.)

A fifth-grader reminded us of the importance of authentic teaching, of putting the students at the center of their own learning and allowing them to discover how to reach their own goals. In a letter she wrote to one of the teachers involved with the Martian Colony Project, she thanked the teacher for a wonderful fifth-grade year. The student wrote, "I learned a lot about Mars. I do not want to ever live on Mars, and don't want to be an astronaut. But after helping to establish and serving in the Martian government, I have decided to be the President of the United States when I grow up."

The title of this chapter is our email address. We would love to hear from you, our reader, if you come up with better ideas or solutions for some of these problems we have mentioned, or others that you might encounter. We would also love to hear about your experiences in general with authentic teaching, learning, and projects.

The teacher I co-taught with in fifth grade became as excited about space exploration as I was. We frequently planned by text, often in the middle of the night. One night I received a text, at 3:00am, to be exact, that announced that she had just read that Mars was going to have rings visible from Earth in the future. I was so excited I jumped out of bed, pulled out my laptop, and researched this. I was totally disappointed to find out that while this was true, the rings, created by the destruction of the Martian moons, were not going to occur for approximately fifty million years!

We shared this story with the class the next morning, and they got a good laugh out of the fact that it was lucky I jumped out of bed to read about this, as I only had fifty million years to get my telescope out and get ready to observe this marvelous phenomenon.

While our love of space, and our hours and method of planning for our project were a bit extreme, our engagement and excitement about our project was not uncommon in our school. When you have this kind of teacher engagement and excitement, all of the problems we mentioned in this chapter become surmountable. -Ellie

Chapter Thirteen

The Journey Continues

Do not go where the path may lead.
Go instead where there is no path and leave a trail.
-Ralph Waldo Emerson

Writing this book was as much of a journey as the journey our school took to authentic teaching, learning, and projects. The birth of this story started in conversations that we had in faculty meetings, in the halls of our school, in the teachers' lounge, and many additional discussions in many different places. We were trying to figure out how to describe exactly what we were doing and why it was working so well.

Initially it seemed simple to explain, but the more we got into it, the more complicated it became. Add to that, not one teacher in our building was approaching authentic teaching in the same way. (If they were, it wouldn't be authentic, would it?)

Additionally, the same teachers were not approaching their authentic projects the same way every year; projects evolved, changed, and ended under the influence of the children in the class. (Again, if this wasn't happening, it wouldn't be authentic.) In picking the title for this book, we pictured a path that we started on and that we are still on. The deeper our school gets into authentic teaching, learning, and projects, the more we realize we may be on the beginning part of this path.

The most important outcome of this journey has been the achievement of our students. It has been phenomenal in ways that can and cannot be easily measured. We have seen an increase in test scores, improved attendance, better behavior, and just a sense of happiness and a desire to learn when you walk into our building.

We have also had tremendous and unexpected recognition from outside the building. "The Lie" was a fantastic example of what can happen when something goes viral on mass media. After being presented by students in the classroom, "The Lie" was later professionally videotaped (family connections with a very talented filmmaker) and posted on Facebook to share with family and community members. From there it took on a life of its own and eventually recorded millions of hits around the world. "The Lie" was recognized by our school board and county council. It was even picked up as a major network news story, exemplifying the power of children's expression in a very complicated world.

One example of this happening at a school could be deemed a fluke. It happens. However, several other projects in our school have received significant attention, honors, and recognition.

NASA recognized the work done by the fifth-graders with the Martian Colony, and also recognized the teachers involved with this project. Two of the teachers involved with the Martian Colony were flown by NASA to the John Glenn Research Center in Ohio to spend a week working with NASA scientists. Of the twenty teachers selected nationally for this program, our teachers were the only two from a public elementary school serving a diverse and lower income population. The majority of the teachers were from middle and high school science programs, private, or magnet and charter schools. The students in most need of an engaging and authentic education were the least represented.

The third-grade opera, "Bigger Than our Barriers" was presented at the Kennedy Center, live on the Millenium Stage. This production is available for viewing at the Kennedy Center website under "Take Off the Mask Kids Opera Company."

A project on the solar system was represented by the students in a dance to demonstrate motion and force in space. A professional dancer volunteered to come in to work with the children on the choreography. When the dance was completed, the students were invited to perform at a TEDx event in Washington DC.

Our first-grade hockey project caught the attention of the Washington Capitals who came to share their experiences and to provide a lesson, hockey sticks, and hockey shirts to the class.

Grants were applied for to support projects and received. Student organized fund raisers for charity met with huge success. Newspaper and magazine articles were published.

Parents attended exhibitions and performances in record numbers. Area mayors, county council, and school board members attended events. Law enforcement and fire department team members attended events and became involved with our students.

The University of Maryland, seeing work on gardening and nutrition woven into our projects, partnered with us to support the learning and to supply extra ingredients, knowledge, and hands.

Even top scientists with the federal government and government think tanks attended presentations and worked with our children. (Full disclosure, we had some family connections here also, but if you have connections- USE THEM!)

While we happen to think we have an outstanding staff and phenomenal students, why was our school having all of this success and getting all of this attention?

We feel that by teaching using authentic projects, by allowing the staff and students to follow their dreams, the student work rose to such an extraordinary level that it was not by chance that our projects were receiving the outstanding recognitions that they were. By using the framework of our district curriculum, and then turning the staff and teachers free to explore at the highest level possible, we were able to reach for the stars.

We hope that reading our book has inspired you to try true authentic teaching, authentic learning, and authentic projects. Follow your passions, listen to your students, risk failure, reach for the stars, and you won't be disappointed with the end result.

AFTERWORD

As Peggy and I were in the final stages of writing this book, I had the opportunity to travel to Scotland with my husband. One destination we traveled to was the Culloden Battlefield in Inverness.

I will admit that my interest in battlefields was usually a quick visit to the visitor's center and then a bee line to the gift and coffee shops. I may have read some history before and noted a few interesting things in the visitor's center, but the limited knowledge I gained was usually quickly filed away and frequently forgotten.

But on this visit, I crawled over every inch of the visitor's center and battlefield. I even took a long hike to see and photograph the battlefield stone monument honoring the Fraser Clan.

Why?

I had recently discovered a wonderful series of books and a television series based on these books called *Outlander*. The main characters were Jamie and Claire Fraser (hence my trek to the Fraser stone monument). I was totally hooked on this series. The genre, historical fiction with some sci-fi added to the mix, was perfect for me.

The extremely talented author, Diana Gabaldon, is one of those gifted writers who makes her story draw you in and live the events with the characters. This battlefield was real to me because I had context from the books. I had been so engaged that I had researched two historical topics central to the theme of the first book, the Jacobites and the Battle of Culloden.

The irony is that an experience that truly draws you in, and gives you context and ownership, can happen all in your own head. I didn't need to go to Scotland to learn Scottish history. I didn't internalize Scottish history because I went to the Culloden Battlefield. I learned and internalized the history because a talented author engaged me.

When I mentioned to my husband how fantastic the experience at the battlefield had been for me, he replied, "Of course it was. You just finished writing a book about why! You had context. You had ownership. It was authentic and it was real. It mattered to you."

Projects

We stated at the beginning of this book that this was not a book of lesson plans. If you are using someone else's lesson plans, your projects won't be authentic and your teaching won't be authentic. We do understand, though, how hard it is to start down the path of creating that truly authentic learning experience.

That being said, we thought it might be helpful to have something tangible to "sink your teeth into" as part of this book. We thought a list of projects that had been used in our building might serve this purpose.

As we started to create this list and describe the projects that had been used in our building, we realized we would need a chapter per project, and that would be an extremely long book. After several attempts to come up with a way to share some authentic project ideas, we decided to go with several lists that could be mixed and matched, and hopefully serve as an inspiration to find that starting point, and some turning points, along the way for that authentic teaching and learning experience.

The first list is a list of many of the projects that have been used in our building. (We tried to remember all of them, but six years into this it was hard to remember everything.) They are not listed by grade level, as we feel that all could be used at almost any grade level.

The second list is a list of ways that projects have been presented in our building. Once you start down the path with a project idea, this may help you and your students find that all-important way to present and share what you have discovered and learned along the way.

And finally, the third list is a list of resources that we have used to enhance projects. Again, a comprehensive list would fill a book, our hope is that this will give you some idea of resources that you might tap into that are available to access and use.

Many of the items on the lists do crossover onto other lists. With true authentic projects, this would and should happen. In isolation, these are lists of topics and activities. Mixing, matching, sorting, and exploring will start you on the path to the true authentic experience.

We hope these lists are helpful. Please contact us with reports of your own ideas, successes, and even failures. (We know how important it is to risk failures and learn from these.)

Best of luck!
Ellie and Peggy

Email:
OneSchoolsJourney@gmail.com

Blog:
The-Educational-Journey.com

List of Projects

Amazing Adventure Stories
Amazing Maze
Animal Books
Animal Museum
Apple Season
Art Gallery
Awesome Adventures
Bake-Off
Book Publishing
Bowling
Car Lot
Car Safety
Chesapeake Bay
Colonial Feast
Comic Books
Communities
Eagles

EmpowHer
Escape Room Game
Extreme Weather
Famous Authors
Field Day
Financial Game of Life
Folk Tales
Game Arcade
Garden Nutrition
Gardening Club
Geckos
Great Migration
Great Pumpkin Race
Groundhogs
Harlem Renaissance
Healthy Meals
Heritage
Hibernation
Hockey
Hogwart's Math Magic
Holiday Card Fundraiser for Charity
Holiday Craft Fundraiser for Charity
Homework
Hope and Fear
Ice Cream Matters
Ice Hockey
Insects
Jewelry Fundraiser for Charity
Judging Ourselves
Landforms
Mammals
Mars
Medieval Times
Military Servicemen Recognition
Motown

Music through Time
Native Americans
Office Redesign
Opera
Osprey Life
Our Own Store
Pets
Pompeii
Pumpkin Math
Pyramids Everywhere
Rainforest
Regions of the World
Rocketry
Rosa Parks Play
Save an Animal
School Rules
Seasonal Fashion Show
Society of Extraordinary Gentlemen
Solar System
Sports Franchises
State Fair
Superheroes
Tea Party
The Lie
The Titanic
Time Capsules
Time Travel
United Nations
Utopian World
Virtual Science Fair
Volcanoes
Weaving
World's Fair

Ways to Present Projects

Student Created:

Animation
Art
Board Game
Bulletin Board
Commercial
Competition
Dance
Diorama
Film
Gallery
Geography Fair
Hall of Fame
Letter
Model
Museum
Newscast

Newspaper
Open House
Opera
Photography
Play
Poetry
Poster
Power Point Presentation
Puppet Show
Recital
Reenactment
Scrapbook
Science Fair
Simulation
Slideshow
Story Board
Story Book
Time Line
Tri-Board
Virtual Science Fair

Resources for Projects

Art Councils
Artisans
Athletes
Bankers
Consulates and Embassies
Elected Officials
Factories
Farms
Fire Departments
Hobbyists
Libraries
Magazines
Malls
Medical Personnel
Military
Museums
Nature Centers

Newspapers
Play Houses
Police Departments
Retail Stores
Scientists
Senior Citizens
Service Clubs
Sports Teams
Television Stations
Tradesmen
Travel Agencies
Universities

Explore…

…create

...organize

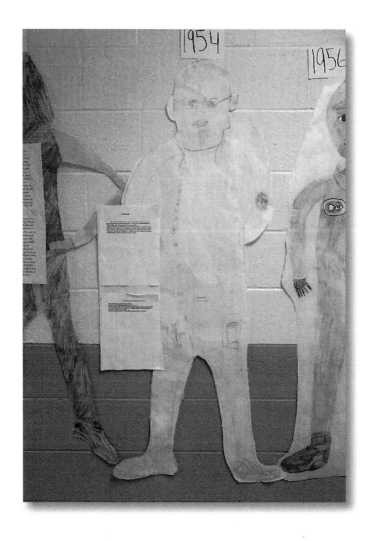

…empower

…enjoy

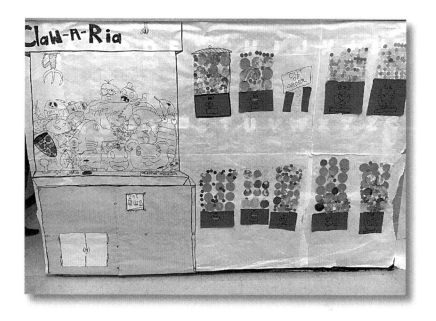

udes health supplies such as tables, computers
age, chairs, garbage cans, shelves, first aid kits
ls, and many, many, more useful things. We ar
king the pod because we think that people need
ysical, mental, And verbal help. We will have a
urosurgeon, a Pediatrician, A cardio surgeon,
uma surgeon, a general surgeon , a dentist, a
ermatologist, A veterinarian,A gastrologist and
any, many more types of doctors that have to hav
least 1 degree in psychology and a Bachelor
egree in other medical discoveries. We hope befor
e go to Mars people could cure Cancer and we cou
e prepared to help with any sickness that comes ou
vay and even the new ones. Nothing is more
mportant to us more than health on Mars and that
can not be possible if all of our fellow MTM Martians
don't pitch in to help with things like the sewage and
the laundry. We need clean water and clean clothes 1
survive. That is our Mars Medical Pod.

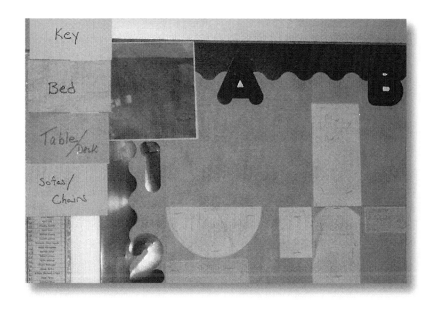

...design

…imagine

...analyze

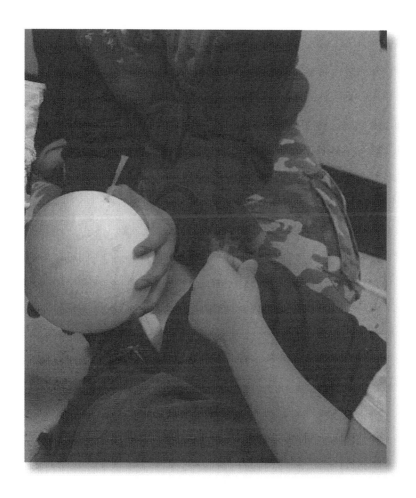

...grow

...combine

...journey

…fabricate

...construct

…advise

…assemble

...replicate

…enrich

…lead

...illuminate

...plan

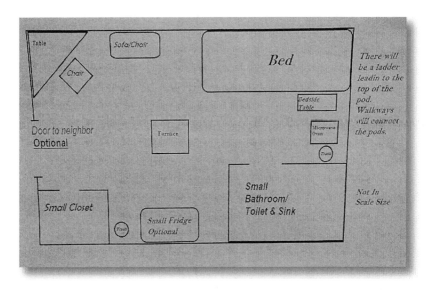

Table

Sofa/Chair

Chair

Bed

Bedside Table

There will be a ladder leadin to the top of the pod. Walkways will connect the pods.

Door to neighbor
Optional

Furnace

Microwave Oven

Trash

Small Closet

Small Bathroom/
Toilet & Sink

Not In
Scale Size

Trash

Small Fridge
Optional

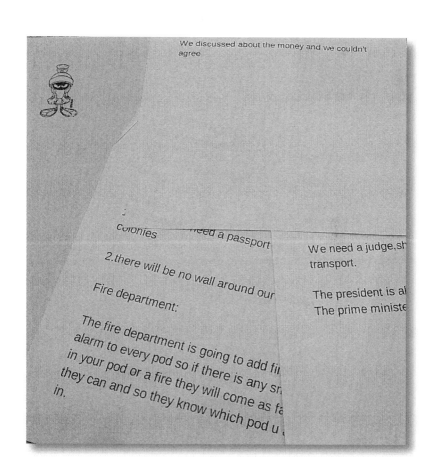

We discussed about the money and we couldn't agree

colonies ...need a passport

2.there will be no wall around our

Fire department:

The fire department is going to add fir alarm to every pod so if there is any sm in your pod or a fire they will come as fa they can and so they know which pod u in.

We need a judge,sh transport.

The president is al
The prime ministe

...record

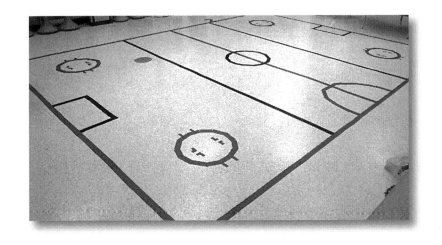

...realize

…perform

…illustrate

...elaborate

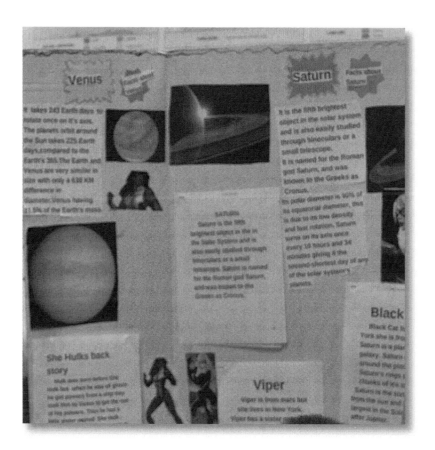

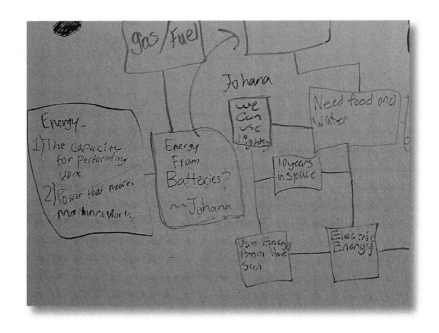

…connect

...reward

…share

…communicate

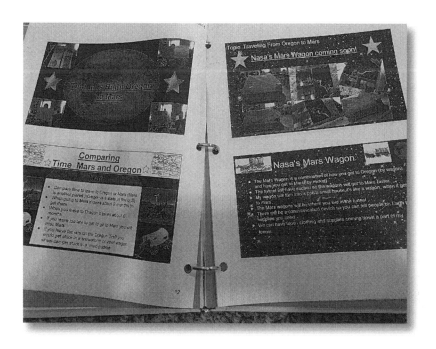

...engage

...Learn

Acknowledgments

This book would not have been possible without the outstanding staff of Stedwick Elementary School. Your dedication to the children you teach, and to your profession, is truly above and beyond. We thank you for sharing this journey of authentic teaching with us.

Diane Adams, Sue Alterman, Christie Anderson, Faith Antizzo, Tiffany Bailey, Alicia Batts, Danielle Bishop, Tamara Bossler, Lori Boukal-King, Vonzella Brisbane, Patricia Bush, Michelle Carr, Joey Collins, Mary Conley, Stephanie Coombs, Katie Craine, Agnes Daniel, Leslie Dent, Gwen Dickey, Dan Dimmick, Cindy Dimmick, Barry Duvall, Kevin Eaton, Mary Jo Eagen, Ashley Evans, Katherine Ewins, Gianna Fogelbach, Darlene Foster, Sergio Garcia, Yenica Gutierrez, Dave Harris, DeAngela Hill, Antonio Hoes, Qunban Huang, Eileen Hubbard, Dewayne Johnson, Rochelle Johnson, Teressa Johnson-Atkins, Linda Judd, Megan Kenneweg, Lenyta Kimbro, Moira LaVeck, Lesley Levy, Matthew Levy, Rebecca Lightfoot, Mirian Lovos, Stacey Lynch, Vivian Malloy-Taylor, Elicia Manriquez, Sarah Martinez, Megan Mason, Jason Massey, Latechia Mitchell, Mary Anne Mount, Jennifer Myren, Laurielyn McCarty, Mary Ruth McGinn, Carol McLean, Tammy Nocket, Melinda Nwoye, Gabriela Pareja-Lecaros, David Pelzer, Renee Pindell, Michele Poole, Jesenia Portillo Elizabeth Portobanco, Tatyana Racosky, Tim Racosky, Barb Reynolds, Yvonne Riggs, Jonathan Rivera, Andrea Schawaroch, Christina Schwinof, Meredith Scott, Jan Shortall, Matt Shuman, Margie Snipes, Paul Stagnitto, Toia Stephens, Erica Stephenson, Kathy Stuart, Pam Taylor, Bindu Tupakula, Amy Weathers, Kirsten White, Feifei Wang, Megan Wilson

A special thank you to the following teachers who met with us to provide additional details about the creation and evolution of their projects. Thank you to Christie Anderson, Katie Craine, Dave Harris, Stacey Lynch, Vivian Malloy-Taylor, Mary Ruth McGinn, Tim Racosky, Barb Reynolds, Meredith Scott, and Megan Wilson.

Tiffany Bailey, words cannot describe your part in all of this. Nothing will ever diminish the impact you made on staff, parents, and children.

Thank you to Greg Smith, Leslie Overton, and Peter Overton for your edits and valuable suggestions. Thank you to Diane Wright for sharing your story with us.

We also want to thank our families for not only providing inspiration and feedback for the projects we were involved with, but for your patience in listening to our trials and tribulations and offering support along the way.

Photographs

Thank you to the following staff members who graciously shared their photographs with us:

Christie Anderson, Kevin Eaton, Stacey Lynch, Mary Ruth McGinn, Barb Reynolds, Jonathan Rivera, Meredith Scott, Megan Wilson

ABOUT THE AUTHORS

ELEANOR K. SMITH is a recently retired special education teacher currently living in the mountains of Central Pennsylvania.

She received her Bachelor's from Michigan State University in Elementary and Special Education, and her Master's from the University of Central Florida in Elementary Education with an emphasis in Gifted Education.

Her thirty-plus year career in special education included teaching in Texas, Florida, and Maryland. In 2013, she was recognized by the NASA Explorers School Program as a Merit Teacher.

MARGARET PASTOR is currently the principal of Stedwick Elementary School in Montgomery County, Maryland.

She received her Bachelor's in Secondary Education and Master's in Educational Psychology, both from Eastern Illinois University, and PhD from Texas A&M in Educational Administration.

Her more than forty-year career has included classroom teaching from the kindergarten level to the graduate level, and administration in both elementary and secondary level, as well as Central Office Administration. She has worked in education in both North and South America.

Contact us at:

OneSchoolsJourney@gmail.com

Follow us at:

The-Educational-Journey.com

91482393R00073

Made in the USA
San Bernardino, CA
29 October 2018